# Jersey Shore

## History & Facts

## Kevin Woyce

Photographs by the Author

*Kevin Woyce*

JERSEY SHORE HISTORY & FACTS

ISBN-13: 978-1546410225

Also available as an e-book

**Website:** KevinWoyce.com

**Facebook:** Kevin Woyce Author

# *Contents*

Kevin Woyce

**Island Beach State Park,** south of Seaside Park, is the longest stretch of undeveloped shoreline in New Jersey— about ten miles of protected beaches and dunes

# *Introduction*

*The Jersey Shore has always been one of my favorite places to wander with a camera, photographing lighthouses and landmarks, and the long, empty beaches of early springs and late summers. With each visit, I became more interested in the histories of the places I was photographing, and in how these histories created the diverse towns of the modern shore. In 2007, I researched these histories, illustrated them with my original photographs, and published* Jersey Shore Facts & Photos.

*I revised and enlarged that book in 2009, retitling it* Jersey Shore History & Facts. *For this third edition (2017), I've changed or rearranged a lot of the images, and updated a few sections. I hope you will find it both entertaining and informative, the perfect companion for a sunny morning on your favorite beach... or for a stormy winter's night when you can't wait for summer to return.*

*Kevin Woyce*

**The Wildwoods:** neon motel signs

## Chapter One
# *127 Miles of Names*

**B**etween Sandy Hook and Cape May, a distance of about one hundred and twenty-seven miles, you'll find some of the oddest names on any map. Driving along the shore, I often found myself wondering: who was *Ortley Beach* named after? What's a *Mantaloking*? Why there is a town in New Jersey called *Rio Grande*?

THE FIRST KNOWN description of the Jersey Shore—"a pleasant land to see"—appears in the 1609 log of Henry Hudson's *Half Moon*. Although Hudson did not name any of our islands or inlets, he did claim Manhattan and the "North River" for the Dutch East India Company. Shortly after Hudson returned to Europe, the company began sending other captains to trade with the natives for beaver skins. (Beaver hats were the height of fashion in seventeenth-century Amsterdam.)

Following the Atlantic coast north to Hudson's river in 1614, Captain Cornelius Jacobsen Mey spied rough waters north of Long Beach Island. He named the inlet there "*Barendegat*," which means "Inlet of the Breakers." Shortened to "Barnegat," the name survives to this day. Besides the inlet, there is Barnegat Bay, the mainland town hof Barnegat, and Barnegat Lighthouse... standing in the town of Barnegat Light.

Hudson never returned to the Jersey Shore. Searching for the fabled Northwest Passage—a way to reach China without rounding Africa—he sailed into what is now Hudson's Bay in 1610. Forced to winter there, his crew mutinied the following spring and cast their captain adrift in a small boat. Hudson was never heard from again.

Mey had better luck. While exploring the lower Delaware River in 1620—the Dutch still called it "South River"—he landed on the southern tip of New Jersey. As explorers often do, Mey named the place after himself, calling it "Cape Mey." When the English took over in 1664, they kept the name but "corrected" the spelling.

THE LENAPE, WHO inhabited New Jersey thousands of years before any European "discovered" it, named many spots along the shore, where they spent the summer months catching shellfish. Some of these names still survive, if only in Anglicized versions. **Manasquan**, for example, is shortened from the Lenape *Manatahsquawhan*, made up of the native words for "island," "wife" and "stream."

Some other Native American names still in use:

- **Absecon** – "Little Sea Water"
- **Manahawkin** – "Good Corn Land"
- **Mantaloking** – "Frog Ground"
  ...or "Sand Place"

UNTIL 1889, **BELMAR**—the name means "Beautiful Sea" in French—was known as Ocean Beach. The town's first hotel, the Ocean Beach House, opened in 1873.

**Brigantine**, photographed from the top of Atlantic City's Absecon Lighthouse. The tall building is the 1927 Brigantine Hotel, now the Legacy Vacation Club.

BRIGANTINE, KNOWN IN the late 1800s as North Atlantic City (there was also a *South* Atlantic City, which later became Margate) took its name from a type of two-masted sailing ship often used by pirates and privateers. (*Brigand*, by the way, is French for "pirate.")

Although legend credits the infamous Captain Kidd with burying part of his treasure here in 1699, such tales are told all up and down the coast, and no hoard of pirate's gold has ever been found.

Throughout the seventeenth century, New England whalers camped on the beach during migration season. Earlier still, Native Americans called the island their "Summer Playground" (or *Watamoonica*, if you prefer the original Lenni-Lenape).

MONOPOLY ENTHUSIASTS KNOW that **Margate** and **Ventnor** are two of the only three properties on the board not named after Atlantic City streets. These names refer instead to Atlantic City's neighbors on Absecon Island... both of which took *their* names from popular seashore resorts in Victorian England: Margate, in Kent, and Ventnor, on the Isle of Wight. (The third property is the misspelled "Marvin Gardens." The actual street separates the cities of Margate and Ventnor, and borrows the first three letters of each of their names: "Marven.")

Some other Jersey Shore towns with European names:

- **Loch Arbour** – Lochaber, Scotland
- **Deal** – Deale, in Kent County, England
- **Brielle** – Brielle, Holland, on the North Sea

LANDOWNER MITCHELL ORTLEY tried to make an artificial inlet between Point Pleasant and Seaside Heights, so ships could enter Barnegat Bay without sailing all the way to Barnegat Inlet. You won't find an "Ortley Inlet" on the map. Ocean currents filled the artificial cut with sand faster than Ortley's workers could dig. But the property he owned is still known as **Ortley Beach**.

IN 1992, THE CITY of **TOMS RIVER** officially recognized Thomas Luker as the source of its name. Although the river had been called Tom's River since 1712—before that, it was known as "Goose Creek"—there were at least three different stories about who it was named for.

Some historians say the river got its name from an old Native American known as "Indian Tom." Others believed the name honored Captain William Toms, an English merchant (and part-time pirate!) who harbored there.

Thomas Luker, who ran the river's first passenger ferry, settled near Goose Creek around 1700 and married "Princess Anne," the daughter of a Lenape chief.

FROM *MYTHOLOGY 101*: **Neptune** is named for the Roman God of the Sea. **Avalon**, which means "Isle of the Blest," was home to King Arthur.

TWO JERSEY SHORE towns, **Lavallette** and **Wall**, owe their names to the War of 1812. Elie Lavallette joined the Navy in 1812. A few months before his death in 1862, he was promoted to Rear Admiral. In addition to the beach town his son Albert founded in 1888, Lavallette has had two U.S. Navy Destroyers named after him, in 1919 (DD-315) and 1942 (DD-448). (The Navy used the original French spelling of his name: *La Vallette*.)

Burlington lawyer Garret D. Wall commanded a company of Trenton volunteers in the War. After serving as Quartermaster General and U.S. Attorney for the State of New Jersey, he won a Senate seat in 1835. Wall was also elected governor of New Jersey in 1829; he didn't want the job, and refused to serve.

**Avon-by-the-Sea:** The Columns, a popular oceanfront restaurant built in 1863

AVON-BY-THE-SEA almost became "Key East," the center of New Jersey's long-forgotten tobacco industry.

Because the most popular resort of the mid nineteenth century was Long Branch, just a few miles up the coast, Avon was still called "New Branch" when Philadelphia tobacco baron Edward Batchelor discovered it in 1897, while visiting nearby Ocean Grove. Intending to relocate his business, he paid $45,000 for a piece of property known as the "Swanton Tract," after one of its owners, and renamed it "Key East." Why? In the 1890s, Key West's main business was cigar making, not tourism.

Luckily, the surveyors Batchelor hired convinced him to build a resort, instead of a tobacco plantation. In 1900, he renamed the town once again, this time in honor of its chief attraction: the 1883 Avon Hotel. Named for the Avon

River in England—William Shakespeare once lived on its bank in Stratford—the hotel is still in operation.

**Inset:** This statue of James Bradley stands on a pedestal in the center of Atlantic Square Park, in front of the Berkeley-Carteret Hotel and facing the Asbury Park Convention Hall.

JAMES BRADLEY CHOSE the name **Asbury Park** to honor Francis Asbury, the first American Methodist bishop. In 1870, when Bradley bought five hundred oceanfront acres just north of Ocean Grove—itself only a few years old—he planned to build a quiet resort for Christian families. Later investors had other ideas, and in 1903, they forced Bradley to sell his holdings, including the beach and the boardwalk, to the growing city.

Bradley was seventy-three, but instead of retiring, he spent his final years developing the *other* resort he created. Shortly after founding Asbury Park, he and business partner William Bradner had purchased another fifty-four acres just *south* of Ocean Grove.

**Bradley Beach:** Centennial Fountain, on the boardwalk

They called this tract "Ocean Park," but soon decided the name was too easily confused with that of nearby Oceanport. It was Bradner's idea to name the resort after his partner—Bradner was too modest to suggest his own name—and so in 1893, the town was incorporated as **Bradley Beach**.

IT'S HARD TO BELIEVE **Wildwood** was once a descriptive name for Five-Mile Beach, but before the twentieth century, thick forests covered most of the island. (The island's first resort, called "Anglesea," was founded in 1885. It became **North Wildwood** in 1906.)

AND HOW ABOUT some of those names on Long Beach Island? We've already seen where **Barnegat** came from. **Holgate** was named for a local family. In the late nineteenth century, variations on **Beach Haven**—the name of the island's most successful resort—were popular. (There is still a North Beach Haven, along with Beach Haven Heights, Terrace, and Crest.)

We can thank the United States Lifesaving Service, a forerunner of the Coast Guard, for **Loveladies**. Beginning in 1871, the Lifesaving Service built dozens of stations along America's shores—about one every three to five miles. Each housed six to eight men, and all of the equipment they needed to rescue shipwrecked sailors.

The Service gave each station a number, and usually named it after the nearest town. Unfortunately, Station 114 was miles from anywhere, and the Service already had a Long Beach Island station. The nearest railroad stop was signed "Club House," after an old hotel, but the Treasury Department bureaucrats who ran the Service considered this an unsuitable name for a lifesaving station.

They looked instead to a map of Manahawkin Bay, where small islands were often named for their owners—including one Thomas Lovelady. Soon after Station 114 was named for Lovelady's Island, locals and visitors alike began calling the surrounding area "Lovelady's."

So when developers reached this part of the island after World War Two, they named their town:

*Long Beach Park.*

The town became "Loveladies" in 1952.

15

Kevin Woyce

**Beach Haven:** Long Beach Island Museum, formerly Holy Innocent's Episcopal Church; built in 1882, the building was converted to a museum in 1976

**Harvey Cedars:** Bible Conference building, formerly the Harvey Cedars Hotel (first built in the 1870s, expanded in 1903)

And then there's this tall tale:

*Daniel Harvey was a seventeenth-century whaler who lived rent-free in a cave near a stand of cedars, which his neighbors called "Harvey's Cedars."*

Sounds good, but historians doubt that Daniel Harvey ever existed. An 1861 hotel advertisement calls the area *Harvest* Cedars. Because this was so difficult to pronounce (try it!), most people dropped the "t". By 1882, the accepted spelling was **Harvey Cedars**.

One foggy morning in 1817, a Tuckerton schooner captain heard someone calling for help. On nearby Long Beach Island, he found an overturned ship and rescued the sole survivor, a young woman, by chopping through the wooden hull with an axe. The names of the woman and of the unlucky ship were never recorded, but the beach where they were found has been called **Ship Bottom** ever since.

AND—FINALLY—WHY *is* there a **Rio Grande** in New Jersey? (Anyone who's ever left the Parkway at Exit 4 to visit the Wildwoods has been there. When you reach the island, the highway becomes Rio Grande Avenue.)

Thank Aron Leaming. His family had owned the area for so long that it was popularly known as "Leamings..." until Aron decided "Rio Grande" sounded better! (You can visit the 1706 home of Aron's ancestor, Thomas Leaming, at Leaming's Run Gardens in Swainton, NJ.)

## Chapter Two
# *Wrecked!*

T he Jersey Shore was not always a summer playground. For hundreds of years, sailors called it the "Graveyard of the Atlantic." Nobody knows how many ships wrecked on our beaches, how many mariners perished, or what treasures washed out to sea.

There were few reliable lighthouses before the 1850s, and our barrier beaches remained largely unsettled until the last decades of the nineteenth century. If stormy weather wrecked a ship on some lonely beach late at night, mainlanders might not spot it until morning broke or the weather cleared... *if* the waves had not already crushed the wooden hull.

According to sailors' legends and sensational novels, mariners also had reason to fear "beach pirates," shore dwellers more interested in plundering salvageable goods than in rescuing stranded seamen.

**Sandy Hook:** Former lifesaving station, used as a visitors' center from 1974 until 2012, when it was damaged by Hurricane Sandy; still awaiting renovation in 2017. The visitors' center has been moved to the keepers' house next to the lighthouse.

It was said that the most opportunistic of these "wreckers" would hang a lantern on a post to confuse captains watching for a lighthouse, or carry a bright lamp while slowly riding a donkey along the beach. To passing ships, the moving light looked like another ship sailing closer to shore—but woe to the captain who steered toward the unseen beach! Because these tricks worked best on cloudy or moonless nights, the men who supposedly used them were nicknamed "Moon Cussers."

THE SITUATION IMPROVED after the Civil War. Iron-hulled steamers began replacing shore-hugging wooden sailing ships. New lighthouses equipped with imported Fresnel lenses, and tended by well-trained keepers, flashed warnings to ships up to twenty-five miles at sea.

Congress created the first lifesaving service in 1849, appointing local volunteers to maintain widely scattered surfboat houses. Starting in 1871, the Treasury Department replaced these "Government Houses" with larger and better-equipped stations, complete with watchtowers and living quarters for paid crews.

By century's end, lifesaving stations dotted our coasts at intervals of three to five miles. Crews of six to eight men, who lived at or near the stations, patrolled the beaches nightly and drilled every morning. When ships ran aground, these men responded as promptly as modern firefighters. If the ocean was too rough for launching surfboats, they shot lines into the ship's rigging with small rockets or mortars. Using a system of pulleys, they then hauled  passengers and crew ashore, one at a time with a breeches buoy—a pair of canvas shorts sewn into a lifesaving ring—or in groups of five or six in an airtight "life car," which resembled a small, windowless submarine.

Kevin Woyce

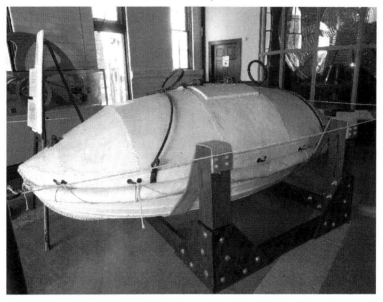

United States Life Saving Service "Life Car," displaying in the former electrical plant behind the Navesink Twin Lights

BY THE START of the twentieth century, a ship on the beach was a rare and newsworthy sight. If there was a resort nearby, a wreck might even become a tourist attraction.

Early on the morning of December 15, 1901, the *Sindia* ran aground at Ocean City with a cargo of Japanese vases and curiosities. By daybreak, crews from two nearby lifesaving stations had rescued all thirty-three sailors and officers.

The *Sindia*'s owners quickly determined that she would never float again. Weighed down by cargo and the incessant pounding of winter waves, her iron hull had trapped itself in the remains of an older wreck buried in the sand. After the most accessible cargo was removed, the ship—and whatever remained submerged in its holds—was sold to a boardwalk entrepreneur, who built a shop over

22

the wreck and charged tourists to watch deep sea divers bring up the rest of the goods.

Not that the tourists needed invitations. The *Sindia* drew crowds almost immediately. Many visitors brought home souvenirs "recovered" from the wreck before her owners arrived to claim their cargo, and for years afterward, sightseers could buy fake *Sindia* artifacts on the boardwalk.

Why the *Sindia* wrecked remains a mystery. The ship was sound, and accusations that the captain and crew had been drinking were quickly disproved. A more fanciful explanation makes the ship the victim of an ancient curse attached to a Buddhist statue hidden among her cargo.

Over time, the ship sank deeper into the sand, until all that remained visible was a single mast—which the September 1944 hurricane swept away. But Ocean City has not forgotten her. A plaque on the boardwalk near Seventeenth Street reminds visitors where she beached, and you can see artifacts from her holds at the Ocean City Historical Museum. You can still buy postcards with her picture on them, and there is even a large reproduction of the *Sindia* on the boardwalk—as the backdrop to a miniature golf course.

**Ocean City:** *Sindia* replica on the boardwalk

ON JANUARY 10, 1910, the *Fortuna* was sailing through heavy fog when she stranded on Long Beach Island. Lifesavers rescued her captain and crew, but could not refloat the ship. After four days, the waves turned her on her side, which is how she appears in countless photographs.

Unlike the *Sindia*, the *Fortuna* was not loaded with exotic cargo. But a century after she wrecked, a drawing of her remains the symbol of the town where her journey ended: Ship Bottom, NJ.

**Ship Bottom:** Fortuna's anchor is displayed in front of the municipal building, along with a tile mosaic of the ship.

IN 1917, THE United States had just entered "The Great War," and needed a lot of ships, quickly. To save money and materials, the Shipping Board's new Emergency Fleet Corporation ordered forty-two "concrete" ships—actually steel frames covered with lightweight concrete.

Only a dozen were built, and none were launched before the war ended in November, 1918. Uncle Sam cancelled the project, and soon decommissioned the entire concrete fleet. Several were sold as oil tankers or freighters, and then quickly scrapped. Only *SS Peralta* remains afloat, as part of a breakwater in British Columbia. *Palo Alto* served as a fishing pier at California's Seacliff State Beach before she broke apart. And *San Pasqual*, grounded near Cuba's Cayo Las Brujas, was once an offshore hotel, accessible only by boat.

**Sunset Beach:** By the summer of 2009, all that remained visible of the concrete ship *Atlantus* was part of her metal frame

In 1926, the National Navigation Company of Baltimore bought the two hundred and fifty-foot *Atlantus*, by now stripped to her steel frame and concrete shell, and towed her from Norfolk to Cape May Point. She was supposed to be the first of three concrete ships sent to the bottom just off the point to form the foundation for a ferry dock.

But in June 1926, before the ship's new owners could sink her, a storm broke her mooring ropes. *Atlantus* drifted into shallow water and stuck fast in the sand. Unable to move the wreck, National Navigation shelved the ferry plan and declared bankruptcy. Although she began breaking apart in the 1950s, part of the ship is still visible above the waves off Sunset Beach, within sight of the modern Cape May-Lewes Ferry terminal.

**Asbury Park:** This postcard, showing "S.S. Morro Castle ashore at Asbury Park" was mailed on September 18, 1934. The sender wrote on the back that from the boardwalk, the ship looks as if it is "just a few feet away," and that "there are three life boats in view." He added, "The traffic was terrible, but it is making a second season for Asbury Park."

IF THE WRECK of the *Atlantus* reads like comedy, the September 8, 1934 burning of the *Morro Castle* was a grim reminder that tragedy could still strike our shore. The popular liner was returning from a round-trip cruise to Cuba when she caught fire near Long Beach Island. Although *Morro Castle* carried enough lifeboats for all of her passengers and crew, the quick-spreading flames prevented all but two from being launched. Most passengers had to jump into the waves to escape the inferno. National Guard fliers from the 119th Observation Squadron searched for survivors from the sky, and then circled them until rescue ships arrived. Aboard one of the open-cockpit planes was New Jersey's governor, A. Harry Moore, who had been vacationing in Sea Girt. Coast

27

Guardsmen, the crews of other ocean liners, and local fishermen saved more than four hundred lives, but another hundred and thirty four people died.

The *Morro Castle* was still burning when salvage tugs began towing her through high seas and heavy winds to New York Harbor, where the nearest firefighting boats were stationed. When the flames spread to her towlines, the liner broke free. Early that evening, she struck a sandbar near Asbury Park's new, multimillion dollar Convention Hall. All through the fall and winter, tourists clogged Asbury's roads to see the blackened wreck. After a weak summer season in the midst of the Great Depression, boardwalk businessmen welcomed the opportunity to remain open, selling snacks and souvenirs. In March 1935, the "death ship" was towed to Brooklyn and sold for scrap.

The cause of the fire remains obscure. Some historians believe it was started by a deranged crewman, who later died in prison after being convicted of a gruesome double murder.

*On September 8, 2009—the seventy-fifth anniversary of the tragedy—the Asbury Park Historical Society unveiled a black granite* Morro Castle *monument on the south side of Convention Hall.*

A NAVY TUG was towing the Destroyer *Monssen* to Philadelphia in March 1962, when one of the most destructive storms ever to hit the Jersey Shore snapped her cable. With no crew aboard to guide her, the *Monssen* washed up on Holgate's beach, at the south end of Long Beach Island. Freeing the 367-foot, two-thousand ton veteran of the Battle of the Philippine Sea took six weeks, four salvage ships, and two heavy tugs.

## Did you know...?

When most of the concrete ship *Atlantus* was still visible, advertisers used the hull as a billboard—first for boat insurance, later for a local restaurant.

The *Morro Castle* was named after the *Castillo de Moro*, a fortress in Havana. For anyone who could afford the sixty-five dollar round-trip fare, cruises to Cuba were a popular way to escape Prohibition in the 1920s and the Great Depression of the 1930s.

New Jersey representative William Newell convinced Congress to create the United States Lifesaving Service.

In the 1880's, inventor Ezra Lake, one of the founders of Ocean City, demonstrated an unusual new lifesaving device on the Atlantic City beach: a wheeled, steam-driven platform that rescuers could drive through the surf to grounded ships. What Lake called an "Ocean Tricyclemor Sea-Wagon," reporters nicknamed the "Sea Spider." The Lifesaving Service turned it down.

The *Monssen* (DD-798) was the second U.S. Navy Destroyer to bear that name. The first (DD-436) was sunk by Japanese warplanes near Guadalcanal in November 1942. Both ships were named after 1904 Medal of Honor recipient Mons Monssen, who had risked his life fighting a fire that killed thirty-six men aboard the U.S.S. *Missouri*.

**Sandy Hook:** Built in 1764 to mark the entrance to New York Harbor, and still in use, this is the United States' oldest lighthouse.

## Chapter Three
# *Lighting the Way*

N ew Jersey's lighthouses have always been among the shore's most popular attractions. Some now house museums, and for those who don't mind a long climb up a spiral staircase, the tallest offer spectacular aerial views of the ocean, beach towns, and bays.

Our lighthouses were built for one of two reasons. Tall coastal towers, such as those at Barnegat, Atlantic City, and Cape May could be seen up to twenty-five miles at sea. These warned sailors when they were approaching the dangerous shoreline. Smaller lights, visible for shorter distances, marked the entrances to inlets or harbors.

The eight-five foot masonry tower at Sandy Hook is New Jersey's oldest light, and the only Colonial-era lighthouse still in use. Built in 1764 to guide ships into New York Harbor, its construction was financed by the sale of lottery tickets by the city's merchants.

Many lighthouses have been threatened by beach erosion, but Sandy Hook faced the opposite problem. Ocean currents continually *added* sand to the Hook, stranding the lighthouse farther and farther from the point it was built to mark. In response, the government built two additional lights in the early 1840s, known only as the East and West Beacons. Until the government assigned assistants in 1857, Sandy Hook's keeper had to tend all three lights—each of which contained a dozen or more oil lamps and metal reflectors! These smaller towers were torn down in 1880.

Better luck attended the forty-foot cast-iron tower that replaced them. The Lighthouse Board moved it to northwestern Manhattan in 1921. It marked Jeffrey's Hook until 1947, long after the brightly-lit George Washington Bridge made it unnecessary. Saved from demolition in 1951, thanks to the popularity of the children's bestseller *The Little Red Lighthouse and the Great Gray Bridge*, the tower remains the pride of Fort Washington Park.

*WITH FEW EXCEPTIONS, mariners considered U.S. lighthouses of the early nineteenth century some of the worst in the world. Most of the towers were cheaply built, and many were too short to be seen from a distance. Worse still, by the 1850s, our lighting technology was thirty years out of date. Invented in the 1820s by French physicist Augustin Jean Fresnel, the Fresnel lens used dozens of prisms to focus lamplight into a powerful beam or flash. Often called "beehive" or "bulls-eye" lenses because of their shapes, they produced a much brighter light than our metal reflectors. Fresnels were made in seven sizes. The largest, called "First Order" lenses, were twelve feet tall and six feet in diameter. You can see three of these in New Jersey. One is still in use, at the top of Atlantic City's Absecon Lighthouse. The other two are in museums: The Cape May County Historical Museum, on Route 9 in Cape May Courthouse, and the Barnegat Light Historical Museum, on Long Beach Island.*

**Highlands:** This seven-ton bivalve lens was used in the south tower of the Navesink Twin Lights from 1898 until 1949, when the station was deactivated. Since 1979, it has been displayed in the station's former generating plant, behind the lighthouse. Originally equipped with an electric arc lamp, the rotating lens produced a dazzling flash—visible twenty-two miles at sea—every five seconds; under certain conditions, reflections were seen up to seventy miles away. Because this was the first electrified coastal light in the nation, the Lighthouse Board hired a former locomotive engineer in 1898 to run the generator.

The United States imported its first two Fresnel lenses in 1840 and installed them in a pair of stone towers on a **Navesink Highlands** hilltop a few miles south of the Sandy Hook light. The French lenses quickly justified their high cost, but the lighthouses themselves were poorly built. In 1862, the Lighthouse Board replaced them with two brownstone towers joined by a matching keepers' house. For reasons known only to architect Joseph Lederle, the new "Twin Lights" were not identical. The south tower is square, the north tower octagonal.

But why build two towers in the first place? Wouldn't one have done the job just as well? Of course it would have. But at night, sailors might confuse it with the nearby Sandy Hook light. By placing two lanterns side-by-side, the Lighthouse Service distinguished the Navesink station from every other lighthouse on the Jersey Shore.

The light in the north tower was deactivated in 1898, after the government installed a powerful rotating lens in the south tower. Given to the State of New Jersey in 1962, the lighthouse is now operated as a museum by the Twin Lights Historical Society and the Friends of Twin Lights. Visitors can climb the north tower, which is lit at night with a small decorative lens, and explore the museum and gift shop in the former keepers' house. The grounds also include the nation's first lifesaving station, which was originally located on Sandy Hook.

**Highlands:** The Navesink Twin Lights

Bust of George Gordon Meade, at the entrance to Barnegat Light.

*George Gordon Meade graduated from West Point in 1835, but soon left the Army to become a civilian engineer. Unable to support his growing family—he and his wife eventually had seven children—Meade returned to the Army in 1842, as a Second Lieutenant in the Corps of Topographical Engineers. After serving in the Mexican-American War of the 1840s, he spent most of the 1850s inspecting and designing breakwaters and lighthouses.*

*During an inspection tour of New Jersey's lights, Meade recommended replacing the towers at Barnegat and Cape May. He also agreed with Jonathan Pitney, the founder of Atlantic City, that Absecon Island needed its own coastal lighthouse. By the end of the decade, New Jersey had three of the tallest lighthouses in the nation, all built from Meade's designs.*

*President Lincoln appointed Meade Commander of the Army of the Potomac in 1863, just in time to lead the Union to victory at Gettysburg.*

**Atlantic City:** Absecon Lighthouse, at the intersection of Pacific and Rhode Island Avenues. The tower is pale yellow, with a broad black band halfway up.

**ABSECON LIGHT** WAS completed first, in 1857. Before its construction, dozens of ships and uncounted lives were lost on this low, dark island. Afterwards, wrecks were rare. But by the time the lantern was electrified in 1925, it was just one of many bright lights in the Atlantic City skyline. In 1933, the Lighthouse Service placed an automated beacon at the end of the Steel Pier and sold the old lighthouse and grounds to the city... for the previously-agreed-upon price of one dollar.

Early in its history, Absecon Light was threatened by beach erosion. When the waves rolled to within fifty feet of the tower's base, the keepers built wooden jetties to deflect the currents. These worked so well that the lighthouse is now two blocks from the beach.

After decades of neglect, the tower was relit and opened to the public in 1999. A winding climb of two hundred and twenty-eight spiral steps brings visitors to the top of New Jersey's tallest lighthouse. From the keepers' "watch room" below the lantern, you can look up into the original First Order Lens, which weighs twelve thousand, eight hundred pounds.

The attached keeper's house is a modern replica, built in 2001 as museum and office space; the original building was demolished in the 1940s.

*When I first photographed Absecon Light, in the early 1990s, the tower was painted white with a red band. At other times in its history, it has been unpainted; orange with a black band; and white with a blue band. Each light was painted differently, so the towers were easy to identify by day. At night, captains identified lights by their "signatures." Some, like Absecon, shone steadily. Others flashed at regular intervals. Some smaller lights shone red or green, instead of white.*

**Absecon Lighthouse**
**Top:** First Order Fresnel lens
**Bottom:** The spiral stairway

THE FIRST **BARNEGAT** lighthouse, built in 1835 to mark the entrance to Barnegat Inlet, was only forty feet tall. It shone so dimly that many captains never saw it, and those who did sometimes thought it was another ship. Meade replaced it in 1859 with a one hundred and sixty-one foot brick tower, which held a First Order Fresnel lens a hundred and seventy-five feet above sea level. His timing could not have been better. Undermined by erosion, the old tower collapsed before the new one was completed.

By the 1920s, the new light faced the same danger. The Lighthouse Service automated the light, demolished the three-family keepers' house, and stationed a lightship—a floating lighthouse—offshore. It was local citizens and summer visitors who raised the money to build the first of a series of jetties to deflect the waves and save "Old Barney" for later generations.

The lens was moved to the nearby Barnegat Light Museum, a former one-room schoolhouse, in 1954. Three years later, the state opened the property around the lighthouse—including a wide beach and the last patch of coastal forest on Long Beach Island—as Barnegat Light State Park.

On its hundred and fiftieth birthday—January 1, 2009—the fully-restored tower was relit with a powerful new lens.

*In 1886, a keeper on watch at the top of Barnegat Lighthouse reported feeling the tower swaying. Nobody believed his story until the morning papers brought news of a minor earthquake in Philadelphia. Due to the tower's height, the keeper was the only person on Long Beach Island who felt the tremors.*

**Long Beach Island:** Barnegat lighthouse, photographed just after sunset.

The aero-beacon in the lantern of the Cape May lighthouse

MEADE'S **CAPE MAY** lighthouse, also completed in 1859, replaced two earlier towers. The first was built in 1823 and stood seventy feet tall. By the 1840s, the ocean surrounded it at high tide. A replacement was built in 1847, but it too was soon threatened by erosion. Neither of these early towers was tall enough to be an effective coastal light, and both were cheaply built and poorly maintained. (Keepers did not receive written instructions until the 1850s.)

The present lighthouse, built partly of bricks salvaged from the 1847 tower, stands one hundred and fifty-seven feet tall. On clear days, visitors who climb the hundred and ninety-nine steps to the top can see all the way across the mouth of Delaware Bay to Cape Henlopen State Park, near Lewes, Delaware.

When the light was automated in the 1940s, its Fresnel lens was removed and reassembled at the Cape May County Historical Museum. The Coast Guard replaced the lens with a rotating aero-beacon, which flashes every fifteen seconds. At night, you can see it from the Wildwood Crest beach, if you step out of the glow of the oceanfront motels and look to the south.

**Cape May Point State Park:** Cape May lighthouse and visitors' center

WHERE BETTER TO build a lighthouse than near a body of water known as Wreck Pond? The shallow pond, between Sea Girt and Spring Lake, got its name because sailors who mistook the narrow Sea Girt Inlet for the wider Manasquan Inlet, a mile and a half to the south, were likely to run aground there.

The Lighthouse Board built a red-brick lighthouse on the south side of the Sea Girt Inlet in 1896. The flashing light filled a thirty-eight mile gap between the Twin Lights and Barnegat Light, and warned mariners away from Wreck Pond.

The Coast Guard deactivated the lighthouse in 1955, after ocean tides filled the inlet with sand. The town bought the building for a library and community center, and then in 1981, leased it to the nonprofit Sea Girt Lighthouse Citizens' Committee. Volunteers restored the light as a museum, and now give Sunday afternoon tours, April through November. Exhibits include artifacts from the *Morro Castle*, and an antique Fresnel lens.

Hurricane Sandy reopened the inlet in 2012. With help from the state and federal governments, the towns on either side have since replaced the natural channel with a concrete culvert six hundred feet long. The culvert has gates that can be opened during stormy weather, so Wreck Pond drains to the ocean instead of overflowing its banks and flooding nearby homes.

**Sea Girt:** The 1896 tower and attached keepers' house, on the corner of Ocean Avenue and Beacon Boulevard

45

**North Wildwood:** Hereford Inlet Lighthouse

THE WOODEN **HEREFORD** **Inlet** **lighthouse** in North Wildwood is a rare example of Victorian "Stick Style," or "Swiss Carpenter Gothic" design. Architect Paul Pelz—one of the designers of the Library of Congress—built five other lighthouses in this style, all on the west coast. His East Brother Island lighthouse, in northern San Francisco Bay, has been a bed and breakfast inn since the 1980s. Several others have been demolished.

North Wildwood was still called "Anglesea" when the Hereford lighthouse was built in 1874. John Marche lit it for the first time on May 11. Three months later, Marche drowned after his boat capsized in nearby Grassy Sound. His successor, Freeling Hysen Hewitt, tended the light for the next forty-five years, and conducted the island's first religious services in the lighthouse parlor.

In August, 1913, a storm damaged the light's foundation. To protect the building, the government moved it on wooden rollers, a hundred and fifty feet back from the eroding shoreline.

The Coast Guard deactivated the light in 1964, replacing it with a rotating beacon on top of a steel tower. Almost twenty years later, the city of North Wildwood bought the abandoned building and began restoring it as a museum. The Coast Guard put the light back into service in 1986, moving the beacon from the steel tower into the lantern room. Today, the restored lighthouse is surrounded by lush seaside gardens.

JOSHUA REEVES TENDED Sea Isle City's **Ludlam Beach Lighthouse** from the day it was lit in 1885 until the government deactivated it in 1927. Previously an assistant keeper at Barnegat Lighthouse, Reeves retired when Ludlam Beach went dark.

Minus its tower, the lighthouse was sold, moved twice, and enlarged for use as a summer rental. Though local citizens tried to raise enough money to buy and restore it as a museum, it was demolished in 2010, to make room for condominiums.

IN 1926, A CREATIVE DEVELOPER built the **Brigantine Lighthouse** as a sales office. After the market crashed in 1929, the stout white tower became Brigantine's police headquarters. In the 1940s, it housed a gift shop, which was eventually closed for safety reasons (the lighthouse stands in the center of the island's busiest intersection). Volunteers restored the abandoned building in 1995, and again in 2013. Although never an official aid to navigation, the lantern still shines every night.

*The New Jersey Lighthouse Society holds an annual "Lighthouse Challenge" on the third weekend in October— an opportunity for lighthouse lovers to visit eleven historic lights over two days. The itinerary includes all of the Jersey Shore lighthouses; the replica of the Tucker's Island Lighthouse at Tuckerton Seaport; and three Delaware Bay lighthouses. For information, visit the Society's website: njlhs.org*

**Brigantine Lighthouse**

## Did you know...?

To disrupt British shipping during the Revolution, American patriots tried to destroy Sandy Hook Lighthouse. Luckily, the tower was so strongly built that cannon balls bounced from its sides, and the damage was quickly repaired after the war.

Naval officer Matthew Calbraith Perry, who is best known for "opening" Japan to the west in 1854, brought America's first two Fresnel lenses from France. (These were the lenses installed at the Navesink Twin Lights.)

In addition to his three New Jersey lighthouses, General Meade also designed Florida's Jupiter Inlet and Sombrero Key lighthouses.

Chapter Four

# *Pirates, Privateers,*

# *And "Rum Row"*

I n the 1690s, the Jersey Shore was a long, dangerous stretch of uninhabited beaches, treacherous inlets, and hidden bays. According to the English government, it was also a nest of French pirates.

Rather than send in their navy, the English sold shares in the thirty-gun *Adventure Galley*. They chose William Kidd, a respected New York ship owner and former West Indies privateer, for her captain. With a crew of sixty men, Captain Kidd sailed off to capture the Atlantic pirates.

In 1699, the Boston police arrested Kidd on charges of plundering dozens of ships during a two-year reign of terror. Two years later, his accusers told a London court that Kidd had turned to piracy because it paid better than privateering. Kidd went to the gallows swearing he was an innocent man, falsely accused.

Treasure hunters have long believed that Captain Kidd buried some of his loot on the Jersey Shore before his arrest. Exactly *where* he buried it depends on where you hear the story... but if the treasure ever existed, nobody has found it yet.

Like the Wild West, the "Age of Piracy" lasted only a short time, from the late 1600s through the early 1700s. Many pirates, including the notorious Blackbeard, began their careers as privateers, authorized by the English government to harass its enemies' ships in wartime. Although most privateers returned to honest trade after the peace treaties were signed, a few continued to prey on whatever ships they could catch. Blackbeard alone

captured at least forty, before dying in a 1718 sea battle near Okracoke Inlet, on North Carolina's Outer Banks. Just a few months earlier, he had landed near present-day Cape May to take on fresh water and provisions... and, according to local legends, to bury some pirates' gold on the shores of Delaware Bay.

**Inset:** Pirate Ship above a row of Ocean City boardwalk shops

DURING THE AMERICAN revolution, colonial privateers captured dozens of British vessels. With the inlets and bays to shelter them, the patriots did not need heavy seagoing ships. Sometimes they simply rowed out from the beaches in whaleboats. More often, they used small, shallow-draft ships outfitted with a few light guns by New York or Philadelphia investors. Locally recruited crews included fishermen, whalers, and small merchants, who knew the inlets and bays like their own homes. For this dangerous duty, the patriots' pay depended on how many ships they captured, and on the worth of those ships' cargoes.

Sometimes the risks were worth it. In October 1781, Captain Adam Hyler of New Brunswick captured five British ships near Sandy Hook, using only his gunboat *Revenge* and two whaleboats.

But British and Tory reprisals could be swift and brutal. In March, 1872, British troops burned every building in Toms River because privateers often docked there. Later that year, privateer Andrew Steel found a British revenue cutter grounded and abandoned near Barnegat Inlet. When he called for his crew and local volunteers to help carry off the cargo, word of his plans also reached John Bacon, leader of a gang of loyalists known as "The Refugees." That night, Bacon and his men took their revenge by killing twenty of the privateers while they slept on the beach. Patriot newspapers called it "the Long Beach Massacre."

A second wave of American privateers hounded British coastal shipping during the War of 1812. One of the major causes of this war was the British Naval policy of "impressing" American sailors to man its warships.

FOR MANY TOWNS along the Jersey shore, the 1920s were a Golden Age. Our boardwalks were lined with grand new hotels, fantastic piers and convention halls, and all the latest rides and amusements.

But it was not uncommon, late at night, to hear machine-gun fire out on the ocean...

In 1919, thirty-six states ratified the Eighteenth Amendment, outlawing the production and sale of alcoholic beverages. The Volstead Act, passed later that year, gave Congress the power to enforce the new laws.

But Prohibition made the United States a "dry" nation in name only. People continued to drink, some of them more than they did when booze was legal. Most cities and towns had their more-or-less-secret "speakeasies," and some of the classiest hotels and restaurants resorted to serving liquor in teacups. In Atlantic City, hotels, restaurants, and nightclubs openly ignored the law.

Most of the bootleg liquor arrived in old sailing ships, which anchored within sight of our coast, just outside the three mile territorial limit. Although smugglers brought all kinds of booze, locals called the line of ships "Rum Row."

When Prohibition began, anyone with a boat could buy directly from the smugglers. Congress "solved" this in the mid 1920s, by pushing our territorial limit to twelve miles. Atlantic City crime bosses promptly took over delivery and distribution. Powerful speedboats dashed out to Rum Row, grabbed their valuable cargo—whiskey was worth sixty dollars a case—and raced armed Coast Guard cutters back to shore.

More often than not, the bootleggers won. Prohibition was never popular in resort towns, and many local fishermen and boat builders profited from smuggling. To make matters worse, most of the men at the Coast Guard stations were local recruits, either related to or friendly with the smugglers.

**Wildwood Crest:** Neon sign at the Jolly Roger Motel

## Did you know...?

The European powers outlawed privateering in 1856.

The only part of Captain Kidd's treasure ever recovered was found on Gardiner's Island (near the eastern tip of Long Island, NY) in 1699.

The Treasury Department created the Coast Guard in 1915, by combining the Lifesaving Service and the Revenue Cutter Service. The Lighthouse Service became part of the Coast Guard in 1938.

**Sandy Hook:**
**Top:** Uniformed volunteers demonstrate how soldiers loaded the six-inch coastal defense guns at Battery Gunnison during the Second World War. The whole process took less than fifteen seconds.
**Bottom:** ruins of Fort Hancock's Nine Gun Battery

## Chapter Five

# *In Times of War*

The British drove the Colonial army out of New York City early in the American Revolution, and then held Manhattan until the war ended in 1883. To guard the entrance to New York Harbor and the Hudson River, they also fortified Sandy Hook.

Only one major land battle was fought near the Jersey Shore. On June 28, 1778, George Washington sent five thousand troops, commanded by Major General Charles Lee, to attack a British army marching to Sandy Hook. When the British counterattacked, Lee ordered a retreat. Luckily, Washington was not far behind. Bringing another six thousand men into battle stopped the British advance, but that night, the enemy escaped to the Royal Navy ships waiting at Sandy Hook. Washington had Lee court-martialed for disobeying orders.

To this day, nobody knows whether the most famous participant in the Battle of Monmouth Courthouse ever existed. She is remembered as "Molly Pitcher," but her real name may have been Mary Hays McCauly. A soldier's wife, she spent the early part of the battle nursing the wounded and carrying pitchers of water to men fighting in the hundred degree heat. When her own husband was wounded, she took his place on a gun crew. After the battle, Washington himself commended her bravery.

THE BRITISH BLOCKADED the eastern seaboard in 1812, but this time, it was the US Army that fortified Sandy Hook, with thirty-two guns and eight hundred men. The British never attacked, and after the war, Fort Gates was abandoned. No trace of it remains.

THE U.S. ARMY RETURNED to Sandy Hook in 1857, to build a stone fort—just as advances in weaponry were making such forts obsolete. Staffed by Union troops during the Civil War, the unfinished fort was abandoned in 1868. In 1890, the Army cleared the ruins to make room for more modern defenses, including the nation's first mortar battery and massive guns that could hit targets up to seven miles at sea.

The new defenses were named "Fort Hancock," after General Winfield Scott Hancock. A veteran of the battles of Chancellorsville and Gettysburg, Hancock ran for president in 1880, but lost to James Garfield.

Although never tested in battle, the fort was frequently updated. By 1919, Fort Hancock's biggest guns had a range of twenty miles. More than seven thousand men served here during the First World War. In 1945, the number soared to a high of eighteen thousand. Late in the 1950s, the Army installed Nike antiaircraft missiles—some of them packing nuclear warheads—to defend New York against Soviet bombers.

The Army closed Fort Hancock on December 31, 1974. The missiles and most of the guns were removed, but more than a hundred buildings remain, ranging from the picturesque 1890s houses on "Officer's Row" to utilitarian Cold War command posts for early warning radars.

**Top:** Abandoned houses on Fort Hancock's "Officers' Row"
**Bottom:** Battery Potter's cavernous interior once held two "disappearing" guns. Steam power raised the barrels above the roof for firing, and then lowered them inside for reloading. Each gun could fire only once every six minutes.

FROM 1874 UNTIL 1919, the Army also used Sandy Hook as the nation's first "proving ground," testing ever larger and more powerful guns on the empty beaches. It was replaced during the First World War by a much larger facility at Aberdeen, Maryland, which is still in use today.

THE FIRST WORLD WAR brought a new threat to the Jersey Shore: German attack submarines. In 1918, the camouflaged *U-151* alone sank twenty-three merchant ships, six of them on the same day.

The United States was better prepared when a second wave of U-Boats arrived in 1942. Underwater nets in Delaware Bay protected Delaware's chemical and munitions factories, and the shipyards at Philadelphia and Camden. Blimps armed with depth charges escorted merchant convoys into New York Harbor. At night, beaches were closed to visitors and patrolled by Coast Guardsmen, some on foot, others on horses, many accompanied by dogs.

"Blackouts" plunged the coast into darkness, to hide passing ships from enemy subs. Lighthouses were extinguished, boardwalk lights were dimmed or turned off, and windows were covered with black curtains. Even automobile headlights were half-covered with black paint, so that they only cast light downward.

**Top:** Nike Hercules anti-aircraft missile at Sandy Hook
**Bottom:** WWII-era concrete gun battery, exposed by beach erosion at Cape May Point State Park

**Cape May Point:** Fort Miles Fire Control Tower #23, now a museum on Sunset Boulevard

THE ARMY BUILT Fort Miles, an elaborate system of gun batteries and fire control towers stretching from North Wildwood to Delaware's Bethany Beach, to guard Delaware Bay against German battleships. The battleships never arrived. Advances in weaponry made Fort Miles obsolete before it was finished, but a few relics still remain. Most famous is the "bunker" that erosion and storms uncovered and stranded on the Cape May beach. In 1942, it was completely buried in the sand, nineteen hundred feet from the water's edge. (Similar batteries remain buried in Delaware's Cape Henlopen State Park.)

To help the gun crews find their targets, the Army built fifteen concrete "Fire Control Towers," four in southern New Jersey, eleven on the Delaware coast. Of the Jersey towers, two were torn down (in North Wildwood and Wildwood Crest) and one has been incorporated into a hotel (you can see the top of it—painted sky blue—rising above the roof of Cape May's Grand Hotel). The last has been restored as a historical monument and museum by the Mid Atlantic Center for the Arts, which also maintains the Cape May Lighthouse. Opened in April 2009, "Fire Control Tower No. 23" contains historical exhibits and memorial plaques, arranged around the spiral staircase visitors climb to the lookout slots on the fifth floor.

## Did you know...?

Atlantic City became an Army training camp during WWII. The Army Air Force trained new recruits in Convention Hall (now known as "Boardwalk Hall"), while a quarter of a million soldiers practiced storming enemy shores on the beach. Many of the resort's most elegant hotels were stripped of their carpets and furnishings for use as barracks. In other resorts, hotels were converted to hospitals for returning soldiers.

Fort Monmouth, named in honor of the 1778 Battle of Monmouth Courthouse, opened in 1917 as "Camp Vail," home of the Army Signal School. Designated a permanent post in 1925, it is now an important center for "C4ISR" (Command and Control, Communications, Computers, Intelligence, Sensors, and Reconnaissance). The first Army radar was patented here in 1937.

Germany surrendered *U-151* to France in 1918. Three years later, the French navy sank the notorious submarine as a target ship in a training exercise.

**Atlantic City:** Boardwalk Hall, photographed from the roof of the Pier Shops at Caesars'

**Long Branch**
**Top:** Statue of President James A. Garfield, on the boardwalk
**Bottom:** St. James Chapel – "the Church of the Presidents"

## Chapter Six
# *The Summer Capital*

L ong Branch—named for its location on the "long
branch" of the Shrewsbury River—began welcoming
summer visitors in the late 1700s. By 1861, the city
was popular enough for first lady Mary Todd Lincoln to
pay a visit. Upon her return to Washington, she spoke so
enthusiastically of the resort that it soon became a favorite
destination for Washingtonians eager to escape the
Capital's muggy summers.

President Ulysses S. Grant arrived in 1869. Given the
use of a twenty-eight room oceanfront cottage by wealthy
friends, he continued visiting Long Branch for the rest of
his life. When not running the country from a rocking chair
on the front porch, he enjoyed swimming in the ocean,
taking fast carriage rides on the beach, and playing Friday
night poker with friends. His visits to the new Monmouth
Park racetrack attracted such large crowds that the owners
placed a statue of him outside the gate.

Grant was the first of seven presidents to summer in
Long Branch; the others were Rutherford B. Hayes, James
A. Garfield, Chester A. Arthur, Benjamin Harrison (who
also had a summer cottage in Cape May), William
McKinley, and Woodrow Wilson.

Elected in 1880 as our twentieth president, Garfield first visited Long Branch with his wife in June, 1881. In July, he was shot in Washington D.C. by Charles Guiteau, whose applications for an ambassadorship Garfield had turned down. Two months later, Garfield's doctors sent him back to Long Branch, hoping that the resort's "ocean air" might help him to recover.

Garfield was, by then, really too weak to travel. To make the trip easier, more than two thousand railroad workers and volunteers spent the night of September 5 building a half-mile track from the Elberon station to the oceanfront Francklyn Cottage. Despite their efforts, Garfield died there two weeks later; historians believe his fatal blood poisoning had more to do with the primitive medical care of the 1880s than the assassin's bullet.

Guiteau was convicted of murder, and hanged in 1882.

Woodrow Wilson, our twenty-eighth president, spent the summer of 1916 at the Shadow Lawn estate in West Long Branch. No stranger to New Jersey, Wilson had been president of Princeton University for eight years and governor for two.

Shadow Lawn burned in 1927. The larger mansion built to replace it is now Woodrow Wilson Hall, the administration building at Monmouth University. In the 1982 movie musical *Annie*, it can be seen as the home of Daddy Warbucks.

All seven presidents attended services at Saint James Chapel, on the west side of Ocean Avenue. Built in 1879 and later renamed "The Church of the Presidents," the wooden building became the Long Branch Historical Museum in 1955. Closed for renovation since 1999, it is one of the last survivors of Long Branch's years as the nation's "Summer Capital." Although **Seven Presidents Oceanfront Park** is named in their honor, and a statue of

Garfield stands on the boardwalk, none of the homes or hotels where our presidents stayed still exists.

## Did you know...?

In 1884, today's Seven President's Oceanfront Park was "The Reservation," summer home to "Buffalo Bill" Cody's *Wild West Show.* Cody's headliners that season included sharpshooter Annie Oakley and Chief Sitting Bull, whose Sioux warriors defeated General Custer in June 1876 at the Little Big Horn River—the battle remembered as "Custer's Last Stand."

The modern Long Branch waterfront is dominated by Pier Village, a Victorian-styled development of luxury condos above street-level restaurants and shops. Completed in 2006, it is named for the historic Long Branch Pier, which was destroyed by a gas fire in 1987. (The ruins were finally demolished in 2001.)

**Long Branch:** Pier Village

**Top:** The old Route 36 drawbridge at Sandy Hook, and the new concrete highway span that replaced it
**Bottom:** Steamship at Long Branch Pier (detail from an antique stereopticon slide)

## Chapter Seven
# *Getting There*

T
he first railroad reached the Jersey Shore in 1854. Its destination was uninhabited Absecon Beach, chosen because it marked the end of the shortest line connecting Philadelphia to the Atlantic Ocean. Critics called the Camden & Atlantic a "railroad to nowhere," but by 1860, Atlantic City had seven hundred year-round residents and hotel rooms for four thousand visitors... and the building boom was just beginning.

Atlantic City soon had three competing railroads: the Camden & Atlantic, the Philadelphia & Reading, and the Pennsylvania's West Jersey & Atlantic. (The fourth railroad on the *Monopoly* board, the Baltimore & Ohio, never served Atlantic City. When Charles Darrow invented the game, he added the B&O so there would be a railroad on each of the board's four sides.)

Despite Atlantic City's success, most shore towns had to wait until the 1880s or later for rail service. Until then, most areas remained undeveloped, or at best sparsely settled. For most people, getting to the beaches was just too difficult. Wagon travel over the state's dirt roads, rutted in dry weather, impassable when it rained, tested the endurance of even the hardiest travelers. And the wagon could only take you as far as the bay. To visit one of the

islands, you had to charter a fishing boat. If there was no
dock on the other side, the captain's duties included
carrying his passengers—and all of their baggage—across
the mud flats to the first line of sand dunes.

And it was not just the islands that were difficult to
reach. When James Bradley first explored the stretch of
shoreline he would name Asbury Park, it was so overgrown
that he needed a machete to hack a path to the beach!

CAPE MAY, WHICH began welcoming visitors more than fifty
years before the first train chugged into Atlantic City, is the
only major resort that prospered with little or no help from
a railroad. By the time rail service arrived in the mid-
1860s, Cape May's years as New Jersey's most fashionable
resort had already passed.

Unlike most places on the coast, Cape May was easy to
get to. The oceanfront hotels were just two miles from the
docks on Delaware Bay, a short ride by wagon. Starting in
1819, regular steamship service from Philadelphia and New
Castle, Delaware, made Cape May the favored resort for
wealthy Philadelphians and Southern landholders. Over
the next four decades, both the steamships and the hotels
grew ever larger and more luxurious.

But Southerners stopped visiting when the Civil War
erupted, and Philadelphians soon discovered Atlantic City.
Besides boasting the largest and the most modern hotels
on the shore, the new resort was only ninety minutes away
by train.

OF COURSE CAPE MAY recovered, and remains one of the
shore's most popular destinations. But in the second half of
the nineteenth century, the fashionable rich were more
likely to summer at Long Branch.

This Monmouth County resort had been entertaining visitors for nearly as long as Cape May. But business really exploded in mid-century, when steamships began ferrying visitors back and forth between New York and Sandy Hook. On the Jersey side, travelers boarded trains for a short ride to the oceanfront hotels. From the 1870s until the 1920s, a series of ocean piers—some of them more than eight hundred feet long—allowed steamers to dock within sight of the hotels.

By the late 1920s, when the last New York steamships docked at the ocean piers, railroads had reshaped the rest of the shore... and were just beginning to face serious competition from the automobile.

MOST OF OUR shore towns were founded between 1880 and 1900, as railroads expanded along the coast. Railroad owners or investors often built the first buildings in town: a station, a hotel or two, and then maybe a beachfront pavilion or an "excursion house," complete with shops, restaurants, and bathhouses. At some stops, ocean piers or amusement parks guaranteed the railroad a steady stream of weekend day-trippers.

But the Great Depression of the 1930s forced the once mighty railroads to limit or discontinue service to many smaller resorts. By decade's end, failing lines were selling unused tracks for scrap. (In many older towns, the tracks once ran down the center of a wide main street; grassy islands or parking lots have taken their place.)

THE FIRST AUTOMOBILE causeways crossed the bays in the 1910s. Most were built so close to the water that waves washed over them in stormy weather, and their wooden toll bridges were often raised for boats. Driving to the shore in the first half of the twentieth century also meant crawling through crowded cities and towns, or bouncing along old backwoods "highways."

Everything changed in the summer of 1955, with the opening of the Garden State Parkway, one hundred and sixty-five miles of smooth blacktop winding from Cape May to Paramus. The northernmost section, connecting Paramus to the New York Thruway, opened in 1957.

Suddenly, the entire shore was within a few hours' drive for millions of young families with new postwar automobiles and money to spend. Following developers' billboards to previously empty sections of Long Beach Island and the Wildwoods, they bypassed aging resorts such as Atlantic City and Asbury Park. Many bought their own summer cottages. The rest would fill the new lodgings that were replacing the grand old hotels...

But that's a story for another chapter.

## Did You Know...?

In the first decades of the twentieth century, some hotels refused to admit guests who arrived by automobile.

The Breyer's Ice Cream Company helped finance the construction of the West Jersey & Camden Railroad. Before the invention of refrigeration, the company needed to make daily deliveries from its Philadelphia dairies to Atlantic City's hotels.

**Top:** Ship decoration, Asbury Park Convention Hall
**Bottom:** Cape May-Lewes Ferry, crossing Delaware Bay

**Cape May:** The Abbey Bed and Breakfast, built in 1870 as a summer home for coal magnate and Senator John McCreary. Used in the 1940s as a Christian Science Reading Room, it has been a popular inn since 1981.

## Chapter Eight

# *Homes Away From Home*

The earliest shore hotels catered mostly to sportsmen, birders and fishermen who didn't mind "roughing it." (Daybreak would find most of them huddled in duck blinds or in small, shallow-draft boats called "sneak boxes.") The unpainted wooden buildings usually stood between the rows of sand dunes, well back from the surf.

Thomas Bond's Long Beach House, located in what is now Holgate, at the south end of Long Beach Island, was once one of the shore's best known hotels. Bond bought the 1820s Philadelphia Company House in 1852 and renamed it Long Beach House. He ran it until 1883, when competition from newer hotels in nearby Beach Haven drove him into debt. Bond died nine years later, at the age of ninety-three. In 1909, his abandoned hotel was demolished and sold for scrap lumber.

Atlantic City's four-story, six-hundred room United States Hotel opened in 1854, suggesting the shape of things to come. In the 1870s, the owners of Beach Haven's Engleside and Baldwin Hotels maintained enormous vegetable gardens to supply fresh produce for their dining rooms. And by the 1880s, most large hotels had their own orchestras or bands, which played morning and afternoon concerts and evening dances. (According to some histories, John Philip Sousa once played violin in the orchestra at Atlantic City's Haddon House Hotel. The story may be untrue—Sousa does not mention it in his autobiography, *Marching Along*—but later on, the "March King" often conducted band concerts on the city's Boardwalk piers.)

Few of these early hotels remain. Built of wood, and lit by candles or gas lamps, many burned to the ground. (Cape May alone suffered four devastating fires in the 1860s and 1870s.) Ocean storms and developers' wrecking balls leveled many others.

Twentieth century developers built grand hotels up until the start of the Great Depression. Spring Lake's Essex and Sussex Hotel, named for the streets that flank its six-story, block-long façade, opened in 1914. Asbury Park welcomed the eight-story Berkeley-Carteret in 1924. And Atlantic City's twenty-four story Claridge, "the Skyscraper by the Sea," was not completed until 1930.

But as far back as the 1880s, wealthy visitors began abandoning hotels for private cottages. In the early twentieth century, less affluent travelers flocked to cheaply built bungalow colonies. Nearly bankrupted by the Great Depression, many of the shore's grandest hotels became military hospitals or even barracks in the early 1940s. Most no longer exist.

The Essex and Sussex closed in 1985. Left in ruins by a failed condominium developer in 1990, the building remained empty until 2000. New owners have since completed a fifteen million dollar renovation, converting the old hotel into one hundred and sixty-five senior apartments and restoring the main dining room to its early twentieth century splendor.

**Spring Lake:** Essex and Sussex Hotel

The Berkeley-Carteret, abandoned to weather and vandals in 1976, needed a twenty million dollar renovation before reopening in the mid-1980s. Renovated again in 2007, it remains open today, a popular site for Jersey Shore weddings.

Casino developers remodeled the Claridge in 1981. Two other Atlantic City survivors are the Dennis Hotel, now attached to Bally's, and Haddon Hall. A 1920s descendent of the old Haddon House Hotel, which opened in 1869, Haddon Hall became part of the city's first legal gambling casino, Resorts International, in 1978.

**Atlantic City**: The Claridge Hotel, seen from the Boardwalk between newer hotel towers

**Asbury Park:** Berkeley-Carteret Hotel

**Cape May:** Congress Hall Hotel

EVER WONDER WHICH of Cape May's elegant Victorian hotels is the oldest?

If not for the 1878 fire that burned thirty-eight acres of Cape May's waterfront, the "oldest hotel" title would probably go to Congress Hall. Thomas Hughes built the original wooden building in 1816, in the rough style of the times: a big dining room on the first floor and rustic bedrooms on the second and third. He called it "The Big House" until 1828, when he was elected to Congress. Critics who believed the hotel was too big to succeed nicknamed the place "Tommy's Folly," but wealthy and influential visitors—including presidents Franklin Pierce, James Buchanan, Ulysses Grant, and Benjamin Harrison—filled it every summer. Harrison even named Congress Hall his "Summer White House" in 1890.

The present brick building opened in 1879. It was renovated in the 1930s and again in 1995, after the current owners purchased it from the Cape May Bible Conference.

Carl McIntire, radio evangelist and Bible Conference founder, owned Congress Hall from 1968-1995. He was also the last owner of Cape May's historic "Christian Admiral," which opened as the Hotel Cape May in 1908. Used as a military hospital during WWII, the Admiral was condemned in 1991 and demolished five years later. McIntire died in 2002, at the age of ninety-five.

## Did you know...?

In 1882, John Philip Sousa conducted the Marine Band in seven concerts on the lawn in front of Congress Hall. The twenty-six year-old bandleader included one of his own early compositions, *The Congress Hall March*, which he dedicated to the hotel's owners.

**Cape May:** Chalfonte Hotel, at the intersection of Sewell Avenue and Howard Street

BRAGGING RIGHTS FOR the oldest Cape May hotel *building* still in use go to the seventy-room Chalfonte (the name means "Cool Fountain" in French). Civil War veteran Colonel Henry Sawyer opened the hotel as an eighteen-room boarding house in 1876. He added another nineteen rooms two years later, and by 1909, the Chalfonte covered almost an entire city block.

DEVELOPER WILLIAM H. CHURCH opened the first part of the enormous Inn of Cape May in 1894, as "The Colonial." Originally a four-story boardinghouse, it had gas lighting and steam heat in all sixty rooms, so it could remain open year-round. Expanded and modernized, the Inn remains one of the most distinctive landmarks on the Cape May waterfront.

**Cape May:** The Inn of Cape May, on the corner of Beach Avenue and Ocean Street

**Cape May:** Saint Mary's by the Sea, photographed from the top of the Cape May Lighthouse

FOUR LARGE HOTELS graced Cape May Point in the late 1800s. Today, only the wooden, hundred and thirty-five-room Shoreham remains, and it has not been used as a hotel for more than a century. In 1909, the Sisters of Saint Joseph bought it for $9,000 and changed the name to "Saint Mary's by the Sea." Except for a few years during the Second World War, when the Army used it for barracks, the red-roofed "convent" has remained a quiet, spiritual retreat ever since. Maintained by volunteers, the building still looks much as it did when the Sisters purchased it. Some rooms were not electrified until the 1990s, and many of the rocking chairs on the porches are more than a hundred years old.

**Cape May:** The Christian Admiral (demolished 1996)

The Shoreham stood a mile from the water in 1890. In 1909, the nuns often rode a trolley to the beach. But by the 1940s, the ocean had washed away forty blocks of South Cape May. The September 1944 hurricane claimed the town's last houses, and the borough was legally dissolved the following year. At century's end, only a crumbling, fifty-year-old sea wall stood between the red-roofed Victorian retreat and the relentless waves.

The Army Corps of Engineers came to the rescue in 2005, widening the beach by more than three hundred feet... to protect the bird sanctuary at nearby Cape May Point State Park.

**Wildwood Crest:** Caribbean Motel (1956), on the corner of Ocean Ave and Buttercup Road. The first of the Wildwoods' motels to be decorated with plastic palm trees, it is now listed on the National Register of Historic Places.

GRAND HOTELS BELONGED to the age of rail. Motels developed from "tourist courts," clusters of rustic cabins surrounding parking lots on the sides of highways. (The word "Motel" is a contraction of "Motor Hotel," first used in California. Early builders often hyphenated it: "Mo-Tel.") Postwar travelers expected private baths, pools, and off street parking. Owners competed by installing and advertising all the latest conveniences: first air-conditioning and kitchenettes, now premium cable and free Wi-Fi.

**Wildwood:** The "Neon Sign Garden" at the Doo Wop Experience Museum on Ocean Avenue

In the Wildwoods, 1950s and 1960s motels were often built in a style that has since been nicknamed "Doo Wop," after the popular music of those years. (In other places, the style is called "Moderne" or "Streamlined"). Inspired by finned automobiles, jetliner destinations, and manned spaceflight, builders such as Lou and Will Morey created a colorful world of curved railings, exotic rooflines, and big neon signs.

Along with all the usual seashore names, like *Sand Dune* and *Sea Shell*, the Wildwoods had motels named for "exotic" destinations, both domestic (*South Beach, Catalina*) and foreign (*Granada, Monaco, Singapore*). Some names sounded ultra-modern, like *Panoramic* or *Trylon*. Others, such as *Paradise* and *Fantasy*, assured travelers that they had arrived somewhere out of the ordinary. Visitors could even book rooms in places named for their favorite cars (*Packard, Bel-Aire*) or hit songs (*Three Coins, Ebb Tide*).

Some other popular themes included: The Tropics (*Ala Kai, Caribbean, Casa Bahama, Hawaii Kai, Royal Hawaiian, Tahiti, Waikiki...*), The High Seas ( *Armada, Blue Marlin, Buccaneer, Compass, Jolly Roger, Nautilus, Viking, Yankee Clipper...*), and The Space Age (*Astronaut, Satellite, Stardust, Starfire, Starlux,* and the *Friendship 7,* named after astronaut John Glenn's Mercury capsule).

The Wildwoods' nonprofit Doo Wop Preservation League, founded in 1997 by the sons of Will Morey, strives to preserve many of the island's distinctive motels and restaurants by promoting their colorful mid-century style as an essential part of the resort's charm. Today, even modern banks and convenience stores look like something out of *The Jetsons*, and the downtown street signs are shaped like palm trees and 1950s B-movie rocket ships. (For more information, check out their website: doowopusa.org, or visit their museum on Ocean Avenue. Built from the 1960 Surfside Restaurant, it's called the "Doo Wop Experience." You can see the outdoor "Neon Sign Garden" from the boardwalk, near the new Wildwoods Convention Center.)

**Wildwood Crest**: Royal Hawaiian Resort, East Orchid Road

**Tuckerton:** 1999 replica of the Tucker's Island Lighthouse at Tuckerton Seaport. The original lighthouse was undermined by the ocean, and collapsed in 1927.

## Chapter Nine
# *Tucker's Island Exit*

R euben Tucker bought the uninhabited island just south of Long Beach in 1765. There he built one of the shore's first boardinghouses, which made his name famous all along the Atlantic coast. The business survived until 1845, when the eighty year-old wooden building burned. Tucker's heirs never rebuilt, but the island once known as "Short Beach" proudly wore his name for another hundred years.

The Treasury built a lighthouse near the ruins in 1848, and then deactivated it twelve years later, because sand had closed the inlet separating Tucker's Island from Long Beach. Rebuilt and relit in 1866, the light remained for many years one of the only year-round dwellings between Atlantic City and Barnegat Light.

The island's fortunes began changing in the 1870s, after the Lifesaving Service built its Little Egg Harbor station a mile south of the lighthouse. Over the next thirty years, a small village developed, as the lifesavers brought their wives and children to the beach.

When the Camden & Amboy Railroad opened an extension to mainland Tuckerton in 1871, developers began building a resort called Beach Haven a few miles north of the lighthouse.

The men at the lifesaving station built their own hotel, the Columbia, in 1875. Four years later, lighthouse keeper Eber Rider opened the larger St. Albans Hotel. Eager real-estate speculators renamed the area "Sea Haven."

For a few years, both resorts—Beach Haven and Sea Haven—were equally successful. From Tuckerton, rail passengers could catch steamboats to either town.

The railroad finally crossed Little Egg Harbor to Long Beach Island in 1886. Everyone in the resort business expected a boom, but Sea Haven's landowners soon realized they had been left out. The railroad ended at Beach Haven, more than four miles north of the Columbia and St. Albans hotels. By 1900, Beach Haven was as popular as Long Branch, but Sea Haven's hotels were abandoned and falling into ruins.

An early twentieth century plan to revive Sea Haven came to nothing, and in February 1920, a nor'easter reopened the old inlet. After nearly fifty years, Tucker's Island was again separate from Long Beach.

Beach Haven was now one of the shore's wealthiest resorts. When erosion began stealing its beaches, the town built wood and stone jetties to protect them. But as many towns have since discovered, jetties built to save one beach may destroy another. This time, redirected currents began washing away the north end of Tucker's Island.

Storms undermined the lighthouse, and on October 12, 1927, it crashed into the ocean. The Coast Guard abandoned its station in 1933, and by the 1950s, Tucker's Island had vanished as completely as Atlantis.

## Did you know...?

Eber and Arthur Rider, father and son, were the only keepers assigned to Tucker's Island lighthouse from 1866 to 1927. Eber relit it in 1866, and Arthur took over when his father retired in 1904. Arthur lived in the lighthouse until the day before it collapsed.

Eber's oldest son, Jarvis, was appointed captain of the Little Egg Harbor Lifesaving Station. (Eber married twice, and had a total of twenty-one children.)

Arthur Rider's nephew took four photographs as the Tucker's Island lighthouse fell into the ocean. Often reprinted in books on Jersey Shore history, the pictures also adorn a wall at the Tuckerton Seaport Museum—inside a modern replica of the lighthouse.

## Chapter Ten

# *Elephants on the Beach*

So you've acquired some undeveloped land at the Jersey Shore. Oceanfront. There's a growing resort nearby, and you're ready to start building houses. Now all you need are buyers. How you attract them depends on your budget... and your imagination. You could buy advertising in the city papers; hand out flyers at the train stations...

Or, build a sixty-foot tall, wooden elephant.

James Vincent de Paul Lafferty, Jr. chose the wooden elephant.

With the help of architect William Free, Lafferty built his elephant in 1881, in what was then called "South Atlantic City." The tusks alone were twenty-two feet long, and it took more than twelve thousand square feet of tin to cover the wooden frame. The total cost—in 1881 money— has been estimated at between twenty-five and thirty-eight thousand dollars.

Clearly, Lafferty expected to sell a lot of houses.

**Margate:** Lucy the Elephant. The building on the left is a gift shop.

His plan was simple. His elephant, which he painted white, could be seen as far as eight miles away in every direction. Outside of Atlantic City itself, by now one of the shore's busiest resorts, there was not much else to see. Dune grasses and bayberry bushes covered the rest of Absecon Island. The only other nearby buildings were old fishing shacks.

Although sightseers could only visit at low tide—a deep tidal creek crossed the island between Atlantic City and Lafferty's property—the elephant was an immediate sensation.

But Lafferty did not invite people to just stand on the beach and gaze up at his creation. There were doors in the hind legs, and spiral staircases to a square reception room lit by some of the elephant's twenty-two windows. Looking out the windows—or better yet, from the open-air pavilion atop the pachyderm—you could see all the fine oceanfront property Lafferty had for sale.

If you liked what you saw, he had a comfortably-appointed sales office in the elephant's head, lit by a pair of round windows—the elephant's eyes.

But in the early 1880s, hardly anybody wanted to buy lots in South Atlantic City. By 1887, Lafferty was so deep in debt that he had to sell all of his property—including his white elephant.

John Gertzen bought the elephant, and his wife, Sophia, nicknamed it "Lucy." For several decades, the Gertzens gave ten-cent tours of the building. They later ran a tavern inside the massive body, and one summer rented the entire elephant as a summer cottage. (There is still a bathtub inside, below one of the windows in the head.)

ALTHOUGH LAFFERTY'S ELEPHANT failed to sell land in South Atlantic City, developer Theodore Reger thought the idea was worth another try in South Cape May. In 1884, he had a crude copy built, forty feet tall with refreshment stands built into the front legs and a souvenir shop inside. Reger called this elephant "The Light of Asia," but his neighbors nicknamed it "Jumbo," after P.T. Barnum's touring attraction.

Though Reger spent about eighteen thousand dollars building his elephant, he sold it to another developer after just three years. Like Lafferty, he hadn't had much luck selling building lots, and "The Light of Asia" was too far from town to attract many tourists. In 1900, the city condemned and razed the ruins.

LAFFERTY DID NOT restrict his elephant-building to the Jersey Shore. In 1884, he began building the world's biggest elephant-shaped building, in Coney Island, NY. Aptly named "The Elephantine Colossus," this one stood a hundred and twenty-two feet tall. There were seven interior floors, divided into thirty-one rooms lit by sixty-five windows and twenty-five electric lamps. After exploring the museum exhibits inside and enjoying the panoramic views from up top, visitors could rent hotel rooms for the night—there was even one inside the trunk! (Lucy is sometimes incorrectly identified on old postcards as "The Elephant Hotel," but only the Colossus was actually used for this purpose.)

Too costly to be profitable, the landmark was soon closed and abandoned. In 1896, it burned to the ground.

**Long Branch:** Another famous Jersey Shore "architectural folly," the 1960s Windmill Restaurant on Ocean Boulevard

LUCY ALSO FELL into disrepair. By 1969, when Margate residents created the Save Lucy Committee, she was facing the same fate as the Light of Asia. In 1970, her rescuers raised her onto a specially designed platform and towed her two blocks to her current home: 9200 Atlantic Avenue. Fully restored, and declared a National Historic Landmark in 1976, Lucy has remained a popular tourist attraction ever since. Inside, you can see a variety of artifacts from her colorful history.

## Did you know...?

Since 1881, Lucy has been painted white, brown, black and—presently—gray.

On December 5, 1882, James Lafferty received a U.S. patent (#268,503) for his "Animal-Shaped Building." Although Lafferty only built elephants, he wanted the patent to cover *any* "animal-shaped building" he might design. Such unusual buildings are often called "Architectural Follies."

**Inset:** headquarters of a Wildwood company that rents beach chairs, towels, toys, and umbrellas.

**Atlantic City:** "Captain" John Lake Young's house, "No. 1 Atlantic Ocean," on the Million Dollar Pier. (Black and white postcard, mailed in 1908)

## Chapter Eleven
# *The Wizard of Atlantic City?*

C an you imagine the Atlantic City Boardwalk without electric lights? Thank Thomas Edison, who invented the incandescent electric light in 1879, that you don't have to. According to local legends, this was just the first of several contributions "the Wizard of Menlo Park" made to America's Playground.

IN 1901, HOTELIER Josiah White III bought an Ohio Avenue lot that was close to, but that did not front on, the Boardwalk. The following summer, he opened the Marlborough House, a large wooden hotel named for the home of the Prince of Wales.

That same summer, an amusements operator bought the boardwalk property in front of the hotel and replaced the old Children's Seashore House with a roller coaster. Josiah and his son John quickly bought the park, tore down the noisy coaster, and hired William Lightfoot Price—the Marlborough's architect—to design another hotel. This one they named after Blenheim Castle, home to the Duke of Marlborough.

Price's creation would forever change Atlantic City architecture.

Kevin Woyce

**Atlantic City:** Marlborough-Blenheim Hotel, on a postcard mailed in 1910. (The Blenheim is the tall building to the left, with the towers and domes. The Marlboro is on the right, with the steep Victorian roofs and dormers.) On the back of the card, the sender wrote: "This gives you an idea of the size of the hotels down here."

First, there was its appearance. All Moorish arches, domes, and sculpted chimneys, the Blenheim would not look like anything else on the shore. Then there was its construction. In 1900, most Atlantic City hotels were still built of wood. When construction began on the Blenheim in 1905, the city still had only a handful of brick hotels.

But Price did not intend to use wood *or* brick.

William Lightfoot Price, born in 1861, was a well-known architect of mansions and railroad stations. Around the turn of the century, he founded the utopian communities of Arden, Delaware and Rose Valley, Pennsylvania. He believed that in the new century, much construction would be done with a material rarely used since the days of the Roman Empire: poured concrete.

Which brings us back to Edison.

Thomas Edison saw every problem as an opportunity to invent. In the late nineteenth century, one of America's biggest problems was a shortage of affordable housing, especially in the crowded cities where most new immigrants settled. Edison believed he could solve this problem with mass produced houses, quickly built by pouring concrete into standardized wooden molds.

Although some of Edison's concrete houses are still in use, this was not one of his more successful ideas. The construction process did not turn out to be as economical as he had hoped... and prospective buyers showed little enthusiasm for his plan to include built-in concrete bathtubs and furniture in later models.

But Edison was as much entrepreneur as inventor. After creating the light bulb, he built an entire electrical industry to make it a household necessity. He produced the first records to sell phonographs, and then opened the first movie studios to supply his kinetoscopes.

So when Edison wanted to build with concrete, he first created the industry to support his ambition. He bought mines and built the necessary factories, so that by the start of the twentieth century, his company was America's biggest producer of Portland cement...

Many tons of which were poured into the Blenheim. Photos of the construction site show mountains of bags, all clearly labeled "Edison Cement."

This seems to be the root of the story—often repeated in Atlantic City histories, but never mentioned by Edison biographers—that Edison himself was involved in designing or building the Blenheim Hotel.

LEGEND ALSO LINKS Edison to another Atlantic City landmark, built around the same time as the Blenheim: "Captain" John Lake Young's Million Dollar Pier. For the last thirty summers of his life, Young lived on the pier in a white, Italian-styled mansion with a mailing address of "Number One, Atlantic Ocean."

Young was one of Atlantic City's most colorful characters. Trained as a carpenter, he claimed to have helped build Lucy the Elephant and one of the early Atlantic City boardwalks. He worked briefly as an Atlantic City police officer, and in 1895, he joined the city's only volunteer fire brigade with Boardwalk access.

In the 1880s, Young teamed up with a retired businessman, Stewart McShay, to operate a carousel in a boardwalk pavilion last used as a roller skating rink. Encouraged by their success, the partners next purchased Applegate's Pier, which had been losing money for its owner since the day it opened. Renamed Young & McShay's Ocean Pier, it became one of the city's biggest successes—thanks mostly to Young's showmanship. He always installed the latest rides and booked the hottest bands and performers. Twice a day, he entertained the crowds himself, naming and explaining all the strange sea creatures dumped at his feet from a big fishing net. (Ads for these "Deep Sea Net Hauls" are visible in almost every picture of the Ocean Pier taken before 1906, when Young moved the show to his new Million Dollar Pier.)

When McShay retired in 1898, Young kept the pier under his own name. After it burned in 1902, he had it rebuilt, bigger than ever.

**Atlantic City:** Steel Pier, around 1910

But the new century brought new competition. The Steel Pier had opened in 1898. In 1904, George Tilyou converted the unsuccessful Auditorium Pier into a copy of his Coney Island "Steeplechase" amusement park. Young knew that to remain the king of Atlantic City amusements, he would have to build the most spectacular pier of all. Like today's summer-movie producers, he bragged to the press about how much it would cost to build: *one million dollars.* Completed in 1906, his "Million Dollar Pier" was so successful that when his Ocean Pier burned again in 1912, Young did not rebuild it. (He did, however, borrow a trick Tilyou had used a few years before, after fire destroyed his Coney Island park: he charged spectators a dime apiece to watch workers tear down the ruins!)

**Atlantic City:** Water Show at the Pier Shops at Caesars (formerly Million Dollar Pier)

Number One Atlantic Ocean became the most famous address on the Jersey Shore. Young loved to entertain famous visitors, from opera stars to presidents, in his elaborate dining room. More often than not, he served seafood he had caught himself.

Thomas Edison is said to have dined there on occasion, and to have enjoyed fishing off the end of the pier with Young. Although he was no longer in the electric lighting business—Edison had sold those companies to finance other ventures—the Wizard is often credited with designing multi-colored lighting effects for the outside of the mansion, and for the formal gardens in front of it. It's certainly possible that he did, either as a favor to a friend, or because he relished the challenge. (In his own way, Edison was as much a showman as Young.)

But the story may be just another Atlantic City legend. Like the Blenheim Hotel, neither Young nor his Pier is mentioned in any Edison biography.

## Did you know...?

The fire brigade Young helped to create was composed entirely of Boardwalk businessmen. Calling themselves "The Beach Pirates," they stored their equipment in a wooden station just off the Boardwalk. In 1898, the station burned while they were out fighting a fire. Young paid to replace it, and provided temporary quarters in a hotel he owned until it was completed. The Beach Pirates disbanded in 1904, after Atlantic City established a paid fire department.

Young's Ocean Pier is now Schiff's Central Pier, filled with shops and arcades. His Million Dollar Pier has become The Pier Shops at Caesar's, a steel and glass shopping mall.

The Blenheim was one of two concrete hotels Price designed for Atlantic City. His second, the Traymore, opened in 1915. Price died the following year, but his fanciful hotels dominated the Boardwalk skyline until the 1970s, when casino builders dynamited them to make room for modern steel and glass towers.

**Asbury Park:** After Palace Amusements was demolished in 2004, the owners of Asbury's popular Wonder Bar repainted their Ocean Avenue building "Palace Green," and decorated it with their own version of "Tillie."

## Chapter Twelve
# *Who is Tillie?*

For several generations of visitors, one of the most famous buildings in Asbury Park was not even on the boardwalk. It was a block or so away, with a lighted Ferris wheel turning through a slot in the roof. Carnival wonders, including an antique carousel and mechanical games, filled the interior. The outside walls were painted green... with two big, grinning faces you only had to see once to remember the rest of your life.

It's all gone now. The rides were sold off years ago, and the Palace was finally torn down in 2004.

All that remains is the guy with the grin and the center-parted hair. Locals call him "Tillie," and you can still find him in the boardwalk shops, grinning on everything from T-shirts to coffee mugs.

You could call him Asbury Park's favorite son... but the truth is, he hails from Coney Island, NY.

"Tillie" began greeting guests at Coney Island's Steeplechase Park in the 1890s. (Legend has it, he is a caricature of owner George Tilyou's brother.) After building a second Steeplechase Park near Bridgeport, Connecticut, Tilyou was hired to revive Atlantic City's failing Auditorium Pier. Renaming the pier Steeplechase, he packed it with his trademark rides and attractions. As

Tillie watched from a pair of towers, visitors climbed in through the mouth of an enormous clown's face. Many even rented clown costumes to wear on the rides—this was, after all, "The Funny Place." (Ladies, beware: Tilyou often placed grates in the floor, with fans underneath to blow your skirts up around your ankles!)

In 1913, when Tillie (and his boss, George) arrived in Asbury Park, the city's most successful amusements operator was Ernest Schnitzler, who ran the Palace carousel house. Two blocks north of the Palace was a competing park called the Flag—which Tilyou promptly renamed Steeplechase, and decorated with his brother's grinning face. George Tilyou died the following year, but Asbury's Steeplechase soon covered an entire block.

Then came the Great Depression, and the shortages and rationing of the war years. Steeplechase burned in 1940, and its owners never rebuilt. By the mid 1950s, the Garden State Parkway was luring tourists to newer resorts farther south. Asbury's political and business leaders tried winning them back with a wave of expensive improvements.

For the owners of Palace Amusements, which had changed hands several times since Schnitzler's heyday, this meant adding a large green "annex" to the old Carousel house. To remind visitors of the "Good Old Days," they chose a most unusual decoration for their new addition:

The grinning caricature of their old competitor's brother...otherwise known as "Tillie."

The murals achieved worldwide fame thanks to Bruce Springsteen, who featured them on album covers and in early E Street Band publicity photos. Before the Palace was demolished in 2004, the nonprofit group "Save Tillie" had them removed from the building (along with a painting of the park's bumper cars) and placed in storage.

## Did you know...?

George Tilyou named his Steeplechase amusement parks after one of his most popular attractions—a mechanical ride that simulated a horse race.

Palace Amusement's "Tillie" was considerably less grotesque than Tilyou's original caricature, which had forty-four teeth (twelve more than most people!).

Ernest Schnitzler designed the Palace Ferris Wheel in 1895. Built at the Phoenix Iron Foundry in Phoenixville, PA, the ride stood seventy-four feet tall and originally featured a two-level observation deck at the top. (The deck was eventually removed for insurance reasons). The Mississippi amusement park that bought the wheel in 1989 has since closed. But the wheel still exists. In 2008, it returned to Phoenixville, where the Schuylkill River Heritage Center plans to restore it as a nonworking exhibit.

**Seaside Heights:** Amusement rides on Funtown Pier, which Hurricane Sandy destroyed in 2012

## Chapter Thirteen

# *A Walk on the Boardwalk*

Like so many Jersey shore favorites, from the Ferris wheel to salt-water taffy, the boardwalk is an Atlantic City invention. The city's hotel owners laid the first one flat on the sand in 1870. Just four feet wide, it wasn't much of a boardwalk by modern standards. There were no shops, restaurants, or amusements. Every September, city workers took it apart and stored it for the winter.

For the hoteliers who financed it, however, the boardwalk helped solve a growing problem.

The shore's first hotels had uncovered wooden floors. When vacationers tracked sand inside, it was easily swept away. But by the 1870s, visitors expected luxurious carpets on the floors of their hotels. Keeping *those* clean of sand was almost impossible.

So, the hotel owners banded together to build a wooden walkway on the beach, where vacationers could take their evening strolls without ever stepping in the sand.

In June 1880, the city built a new, fourteen foot-wide boardwalk. Instead of laying flat on the sand, this one rested on eighteen-inch pilings. Like the original, it had no railings, and still went into storage every September.

Kevin Woyce

**Top:** south end of the two-mile Wildwood boardwalk
**Bottom:** Seaside Heights boardwalk, photographed in 2013

But for the first time, the city allowed businesses along the walk. Shops and restaurants had to be ten away, and bathhouses could not be closer than fifteen feet. Because these structures had to withstand winter storms, many owners raised them high on wooden pilings. Wooden ramps connected them to the boardwalk.

Atlantic City built its first "permanent" boardwalk in 1884. Two miles long, it was probably the most unusual *looking* boardwalk in history. Pilings raised it five feet above the sand, except at the ends of the city's streets. There, ramps lifted the boardwalk into bridges, high enough for vacationers to ride their horses underneath to the beach (Horses were not banned from the beach until 1892, and then only during posted "bathing hours").

This was also one of the most cluttered boardwalks in history. There were businesses on both sides, and some sections were even covered with roofs... until September 9, 1889, when a hurricane blew them all away.

The city rebuilt, of course, and in time for the 1890 season. Except for a handful of piers, businesses were restricted to the landward side. Raising the entire walk to a height of ten feet eliminated the odd "bridges" at the street ends... and finally forced the city to install railings.

The modern Atlantic City Boardwalk debuted in June 1896. Widened to forty feet, it was now supported by a steel frame rather than wood pilings. On opening day, it was designated an official city street, which is why its name has been capitalized ever since. No other boardwalk shares this distinction.

The West Jersey & Atlantic Railroad built Atlantic City's first pier in 1880. A storm destroyed it later that same year, and the railroad never rebuilt.

The city's second pier builder, Colonel George Howard, did not fare much better. He opened his first pier in July 1881. Critics called it "Howard's Folly," and Mother Nature seemed to agree. In September, a storm washed it away. Howard tried again two years later, only to have his second pier wrecked by a January storm. Like the West Jersey & Atlantic, Howard decided not to rebuild. The ruins stood until 1891, when a company owned by John Lake Young demolished them.

Atlantic City's most famous pier opened on June 18, 1898. Stretching seventeen-hundred and eighty feet into the Atlantic, the Steel Pier was promoted as "The Showplace of the Nation." From the 1890s until the 1970s, all the most popular entertainers and musical acts played there—along with such curiosities as a high-diving horse and a water-skiing dog. Four Miss Americas were crowned on the pier (1935-1938), and for more than forty years, General Motors displayed its newest cars there (1926-1968). But the Steel Pier closed in 1976, and fire destroyed the original wooden-decked structure in 1982. In 1993, a smaller, concrete version opened as an amusement park opposite the Taj Mahal casino.

William Somers built the city's first "Ferris" wheel (he called it an "observation roundabout") in 1891. Two years later, George Washington Gales Ferris, Jr. designed a much larger one for Chicago's World Columbian Exposition. Convinced that Ferris had stolen the idea from him, Somers built a second wheel just outside the fairgrounds.

Somers also designed a "roundabout" for Asbury Park. (Author Stephen Crane called its riders "maniacs," while area hotel owners complained about the ashes from its steam engine.) After his original Atlantic City wheel burned, Somers replaced it with an attention-getting *double* wheel—two sets of carriages rotating side-by-side.

Ferris died in 1896, at the age of thirty-seven. His wheel was moved to St. Louis for the 1904 Louisiana Purchase Exposition, and dynamited after the fair closed.

*The tradition of bringing boxes of saltwater taffy back from the shore for family and friends began around 1880 in Atlantic City. Joseph Fralinger probably did not invent the candy, as is sometimes claimed. But he was the*

*first merchant to package it in souvenir boxes, instead of selling it loose. The company he started is still in business, along with that of his chief rival, Enoch James.*

*Jersey Shore taffy does not—and never did—contain any salt water. (The main ingredients are sugar, cornstarch, and butter.) So where did the name come from? The usual explanation is that the owner of a boardwalk candy shop found his store flooded after a storm. When he advertised his surviving stock as* "Salt Water Taffy," *the candy sold so well that the name has been used ever since.*

**Inset:** "Salt Water Taffy" sculpture outside a candy store on Long Beach Island.

Kevin Woyce

**Asbury Park:** Paramount Theater (left) and Convention Hall

THE BOARDWALK IDEA spread quickly along the shore. Asbury Park built one in 1877, Point Pleasant and Ocean City in 1880.

Until the late 1920s, Asbury Park's mile-long boardwalk was lined with old wooden pavilions, including a sprawling 1903 "Casino" on the Ocean Grove border. (Asbury's Casino was never a gambling hall. In the late nineteenth and early twentieth centuries, the word could refer to any large public building.) Fires destroyed most of these structures in 1927 and 1928.

To replace them, the city hired New York architects Whitney Warren and Charles Wetmore, designers of New York's Grand Central Terminal (1913) and the nearby Berkeley-Carteret Hotel. Their spectacular designs wound up costing Asbury more than four and a half million dollars, right at the start of the Great Depression.

**Asbury Park:** The Casino. The tower belongs to the 1920s heating plant, which served the Casino and the Convention Hall / Paramount Theater complex four blocks away. When the beaches were segregated, this building also housed separate concessions for African American visitors.

The Paramount Theater / Convention Hall complex was "air conditioned" by fans blowing across large blocks of ice in an insulated basement. In colder weather, a pipe underneath the boardwalk brought heat from a plant located four blocks to the south, behind the Casino. The plant's concrete, Art-Deco smokestack remains one of Asbury Park's most visible landmarks.

Like much of Asbury Park, these historic structures fell into disrepair in the latter half of the twentieth century. Since 2000, extensive renovations and new shops and restaurants have brought the Convention Hall / Paramount Theater complex, and much of the boardwalk, back to life.

**Asbury Park:** The 1962 Fifth Avenue Pavilion, home for several decades to a Howard Johnson's restaurant, now houses a cafe.

Half of the Casino has been demolished. The carousel house still stands, alongside the hangar-like boardwalk arcade. But the pier was too far gone to save. Only the limestone decorations remain, stored away for when the city replaces the landmark.

The Casino carousel house is now used for art exhibits and theater-in-the-round. But from 1932 to 1990, it housed the last hand-carved carousel manufactured by the Philadelphia Toboggan Company of Hatfield, Pennsylvania. Although the original wooden horses were sold in the 1980s, the ride survives at Family Kingdom Park in Myrtle Beach, South Carolina. Like most modern carousels, it has fiberglass animals.

The wooden horses from the Palace Amusements Carousel were also sold in the 1980s. The rest of the ride was later sold to an amusement park in Mississippi, which has since closed.

**Point Pleasant:** Commercial fishing boats, a sightseeing vessel, and small pleasure craft in the busy harbor, with the Coast Guard station in the background.

BEFORE OPENING JENKINSON'S Pavilion on the Point Pleasant Beach boardwalk in 1928, Charles Jenkinson operated soda fountains in Asbury Park and Ocean Grove. By the time he died in 1937, his Point Pleasant empire included a dance hall, a swimming pool, and a miniature golf course. His son Orlo added kiddie rides in the 1940s, and then a miniature train on the beach. Although the Jenkinson family sold the business in the 1970s, their name remains virtually synonymous with "Point Pleasant." The Pavilion was rebuilt after a fire in 1990, and again after Hurricane Sandy in 2012.

**Ocean City:** Wonderland Pier carousel

**Ocean City:** Ferris wheel at Gillian's Wonderland Pier

DAVID GILLIAN BEGAN his career on the Ocean City boardwalk in 1914, as a dance band drummer. In 1930, he opened his Fun Deck amusement park, which featured a Ferris wheel and a carousel. Sixty years later, he celebrated his hundredth birthday by donating one of the carousel's horses to the Ocean City Historical Museum.

In 1956, David's son Roy opened Wonderland Pier amusement park. Today it has a giant Ferris wheel, visible from the Garden State Parkway, and one of the last two hand-carved carousels on the shore: a 1926 Philadelphia Toboggan Company masterpiece that the Gillian family bought from a Pennsylvania amusement park in 1972.

**Ocean City:** Music Pier.

David Gillian died in 1993 (he was a hundred and two), but his children and grandchildren still operate both amusement parks, along with many other boardwalk attractions. (And in the 1980s, Roy Gillian served as the town's mayor.)

The modern Ocean City boardwalk opened on the city's fiftieth birthday: July 4, 1929. Its centerpiece was a new, Spanish-styled Music Pier, which remains the summertime home of the Ocean City Pops orchestra. Fire had destroyed part of the original boardwalk, and many of its attractions, in October 1927.

The painting of a blue whale and her calf on the north side of the boardwalk's Eighth Avenue Fudge Kitchen is a hundred and thirty-five feet long and thirty-two feet high. Marine artist David Dunleavy spent five days painting it in October, 2007. He has also painted sea life murals at the Stone Harbor Mall and at the Washington Street Mall in Cape May.

FOR NEARLY HALF a century, Beach Haven had one of the shore's most elegant boardwalks. Never a busy commercial strip, it began in 1896 as a four block pathway connecting the bathhouses in front of the resort's two biggest hotels, the Engleside and the Baldwin (the Engleside was built in 1873 and demolished in 1943; the Baldwin, which opened in 1883, burned in September, 1960.

The town quickly replaced this first walk with a half-mile promenade raised on wooden pilings. In 1917, the boardwalk was extended to more than a mile in length, with benches on both sides and a gas lamp at the end of every block. Entrepreneurs opened a handful of shops, and a single arcade, in the 1920s and '30s.

The September, 1944 hurricane—one of the most destructive ever to hit the Shore—wrecked the entire boardwalk and most of its businesses. Rather than try to rebuild, Beach Haven sold all the wood it could salvage to Atlantic City, which used it to rebuild its own badly-damaged Boardwalk.

Among those who lost their businesses to the storm were Nat and Betty Ewer. They reopened their popular gift shop a few years later aboard the *Lucy Evelyn*, a 1917 schooner they purchased, restored, and beached on the bay shore. Forced to rebuild yet again after fire claimed the *Lucy Evelyn* in 1972, the Ewers created Schooner's Wharf, still one of Long Beach Island's most popular shopping centers.

**Seaside Heights:** Casino Pier Carousel and 1927 Wurlitzer Military Band Organ

IT TOOK TWO master carvers, William Dentzel and Charles Looff, to create the fifty-eight animals for the 1910 Casino Pier carousel (Along with the horses, you'll find a lion, a tiger, a donkey, and two camels). The carousel ran at an amusement park in Burlington, NJ until 1932, when the Seaside Heights Casino was built to house it.

In the 1980s, the Pier's owners considered selling the wooden figures. Dr. Floyd Moreland, a classics professor who rode the carousel as a child, volunteered to restore them instead. Thanks to him, the ride remained one of the Jersey Shore's "must-see" attractions for another three decades. In addition to the beautifully restored animals, it had the only operating Wurlitzer Military Band Organ in New Jersey... and was decorated with more than two thousand electric lights.

In 2015, the owners of Casino Pier traded the carousel to the city, for an acre of beach on which they have built a new roller coaster, Ferris wheel, and other rides to replace those destroyed by Hurricane Sandy. The carousel will remain in storage until the city builds it a new home.

Seaside Heights has had a mile-long boardwalk since 1921, but the busy midway and amusement piers did not develop until the 1950s. During the Second World War, the boardwalk became a popular destination for soldiers on leave; afterwards, many of them returned year after year with their families.

**Wildwood:** The Great White, a wood-tracked, steel-framed roller coaster at Morey's Adventure Pier

WILDWOOD BUILT ITS first boardwalk in 1895. By the 1920s, its attractions rivaled those of Atlantic City—you could even stop to watch alligator wrestling!

Brothers Lou and Will Morey were already successful motel builders when they turned their attention to the Wildwood boardwalk. They built Surfside Pier, the island's first water park, in 1969. Other attractions quickly followed, including a popular King Kong airplane ride. After opening their first "Morey's Pier" in 1974, they began buying older competitors, including Marine Pier, a boardwalk landmark since 1918.

King Kong is no more. The hollow, forty-foot statue fell to pieces in 1980, when workers tried to move it to New York for repairs. But Morey's Piers—they own four—can still boast the Wildwoods' most spectacular landmarks.

The hundred and fifty-foot Ferris wheel they installed in 1985 is still the tallest on the Jersey Shore. The "Great Nor'easter" roller coaster soars to a hundred and fifteen feet, and the "Great White" is the island's only wooden coaster.

The Boardwalk Mall was originally a wooden theater on Atlantic Avenue. It was moved to the boardwalk in 1921, rebuilt with concrete blocks in the 1940s, and converted to a mall in 1977. In 1993, marine artist Wyland painted two life-size humpback whales on the north outside wall. Two hundred and twenty feet long, and thirty feet high, this is the forty-third of the hundred "Whaling Walls" Wyland has painted worldwide, and the only one located in New Jersey.

Wildwood resident Floss Stingel recorded the words "watch the tramcar, please" in 1971. But these blue and yellow, battery-powered trains have been carrying visitors up and down the two-mile boardwalk since June 1949... and five of them have been rolling since 1939, when they were built for the New York World's Fair. Running at their top speed of five miles per hour, each tramcar can make a round trip once an hour. Every summer, they carry about half a million visitors.

## Did you know...?

Early attractions on the Atlantic City Boardwalk included human oddities—two-headed women were always popular—and theatrical recreations of natural disasters, including the 1889 Johnstown Flood. An early "thrill ride" let visitors pedal bicycles attached to elevated tracks on the beach.

Twelve years before the Steel Pier opened, Atlantic City had an "Iron Pier." Henry John Heinz bought it in 1898, to showcase his company's "57 Varieties" of pickles, ketchup, and other food products. Like many of Atlantic City's early piers, this one no longer exists. The September 1944 hurricane damaged it so badly that the Heinz Company chose to demolish it rather than rebuild.

In its last decade, the Long Branch Pier's most popular attraction was the three-story "Haunted Mansion." Built in 1977, the Mansion had been built by the owners of "Brigantine Castle," which had opened a year earlier on an ocean pier in Brigantine. Damaged by a 1982 storm, the Castle closed in 1984 and burned in 1987—the same year fire claimed the Long Branch Pier. Though fondly remembered, neither attraction was ever rebuilt.

**Atlantic City:** gargoyle head displayed outside the Atlantic City Historical Museum on Garden Pier. Built in 1913 at the foot of New Jersey Avenue, the seven-hundred foot ocean pier is also home to the Atlantic City Art Center.

**Seaside Heights:** 2009 photograph of the popular "Sky Ride" along the Boardwalk, one of the many attractions that had to be rebuilt after Hurricane Sandy

## Chapter Fourteen
# *Jersey Shore Odds and Ends*

At early shore resorts, men and women were not allowed in the ocean at the same time. Alternating red and white flags let everyone know whose turn it was.

For many nineteenth century visitors, a walk on the beach was more than just a pleasant way to waste a morning. In an age when Americans credited "Sea Air" with more restorative powers than most patent medicines, doctors often "prescribed" a few weeks at one of the shore's resorts.

Many early postcards were hand colored—usually overseas, by people who had never seen the Jersey Shore.

Automobile pioneers once demonstrated their latest inventions on Cape May's Beach. Twenty thousand spectators attended one 1905 race, in which both Henry Ford and Louis Chevrolet competed. (Ford came in last.)

Ohio's Mary Katherine Campbell won Atlantic City's Miss America pageant in 1922 *and* 1923, making her the only contestant who ever won more than once. Artist Norman Rockwell was one of the 1922 judges.

**Ocean Grove:** the Great Auditorium

**Ocean Grove**
**Top:** summer tent colony
**Bottom**: restored gingerbread-style cottages

137

Ocean Grove's Great Auditorium, built in 1894, seats nine thousand people. In 1908, the front of the building was extended to make room for an organ with eight thousand pipes—then the largest in the world. In contrast to such grandeur, there are still more than a hundred tents surrounding the Auditorium. Some have been owned by the same families for generations. If you want to rent one during the summer, there's a twenty-year waiting list!

Until 1981, no vehicles were allowed in Ocean Grove on Sundays—and it didn't matter who you were. Even President Grant (a notoriously fast driver) had to get out of his carriage and walk when he drove down from Long Branch. Such laws were once common along the shore. Ocean City did not abolish its Sunday closing laws until 1986. Even Atlantic City once had Sunday "blue" laws... which most business owners and visitors ignored.

Charles Landis, who started the city of Vineland, brought big plans to the shore in 1880. Ludlam's Beach, named for an early settler, was then unoccupied but for two lifesaving stations and a small lighthouse. Certain that the West Jersey & Seashore Railroad would soon reach the island—it finally arrived in 1892—Landis mapped out a resort like no other: a nineteenth century American Venice, with canals instead of streets. It was never built. But not long after Landis's grandiose plans collapsed, the new Sea Isle City Improvement Company began building one of the shore's most popular resorts.

Simon Lake, grandson of one of the founders of Ocean City, built a small, wooden submarine in 1895, which he called *Argonaut, Jr.* After testing it in the Shrewsbury River, he built a larger submarine of iron in Baltimore. Calling this one *Argonaut*, he tested it in Chesapeake Bay, and then in 1898, sailed it up the Atlantic Coast to Sandy Hook Bay. Jules Verne—whose novel *20,000 Leagues Under the Sea* had fired Lake's imagination two decades before—sent his congratulations. Between 1909 and 1922, Lake's company built thirty-three attack submarines for the US Navy. Unlike his earlier prototypes, which had been designed for exploring the seafloor, the naval subs were not equipped with wheels.

Stephen Crane's family moved to Asbury Park when he was thirteen. While still in his teens, he began writing satirical articles about Asbury and neighboring Ocean Grove for the *New York Tribune*. Crane left Asbury in 1892 to write for the *New York Press*, and published his masterpiece, *The Red Badge of Courage*, two years later. He died of tuberculosis in 1900, at the age of twenty-nine.

Bill Haley and His Comets gave their first public performance of *Rock Around The Clock* at Wildwood's HofBrau Hotel in 1954. Since 2004, this event has been celebrated every October as part of Wildwood's "Fabulous Fifties Weekend."

*Kevin Woyce*

**Wildwood Crest:** sunrise over the ocean...

...and sunset over the bay

*Kevin Woyce*

## Selected Bibliography

Cain, Tim. Peck's Beach: A Pictorial History of Ocean City New Jersey. Harvey Cedars: Down the Shore, 1988.

DeWire, Elinor. Lighthouses of the Mid-Atlantic Coast. Stillwater: Voyageur Press, 2002.

Futrell, Jim. Amusement Parks of New Jersey. Mechanicsburg: Stackpole Books, 2004.

Holland, F. Ross, Jr. Great American Lighthouses. Washington, DC: The Preservation Press, 1994.

Levi, Vicki Gold and Eisenberg, Lee. Atlantic City: 125 Years of Ocean Madness. New York: Clarkson N. Potter, Inc., 1979.

Lloyd, John Bailey. Eighteen Miles of History on Long Beach Island. Harvey Cedars: Down the Shore, 1994.

Lloyd. Six Miles at Sea. Harvey Cedars: Down the Shore, 1990.

McMahon, William. So Young... So Gay! The Story of the Boardwalk 1870-1970. Atlantic City: Atlantic City Press, 1970.

Methot, June. Up & Down The Beach. Navesink: Whip Publishers, 1988.

Pike, Helen-Chantal. Asbury Park's Glory Days. New Brunswick: Rutger's University Press, 2005.

Roberts, Russell and Youmans, Rich. Down the Jersey Shore. New Brunswick: Rutgers University Press, 2000.

Salvini, Emil. Boardwalk Memories: Tales of the Jersey Shore. Guilford: Globe Pequot Press, 2005.

Seibold, David and Adams, Charles J. III. Shipwrecks Off Ocean City. Wyomissing Hills: Exeter House Books, 1986.

Seibold and Adams. Shipwrecks and Legends 'Round Cape May. Reading: Exeter House Books, 1987.

## About the Author

KEVIN WOYCE is an author, photographer, and lecturer, specializing in regional history. A lifelong resident of the Garden State, he grew up in East Rutherford—the eldest of fifteen siblings—and now lives in Lyndhurst.

His books include:

*Liberty: An Illustrated History*

*Niagara: The Falls and the River*

*New Jersey State Parks: History & Facts*

**Website:** KevinWoyce.com

**Facebook:** Kevin Woyce Author

64563215R00081

Made in the USA
Lexington, KY
12 June 2017